"Many Christian resources focus either on b: of deep personal life transformation or on l very flattened understanding of the gospel. World Harvest has drawn upon their history of rich gospel-based training to produce a series that targets real-life transformation grounded in a robust, grace-based theology. Only a resource saturated in the gospel can lead to the kind of meaningful life change promised to us in the Bible, and I am thrilled to see such a resource now available."

> **Rev. David H. Kim**, Director of the Gotham Initiative, Redeemer Presbyterian Church, NYC

"I love the series of small group resources, *Gospel Identity*, *Gospel Growth*, and *Gospel Love*. They are theologically rich, but not stuffy; practical, but not pragmatic. They are life-transforming resources that will be used to transform communities on mission with the gospel."

> **Scott Thomas**, Pastor of Pastoral Development, The Journey Church

"This study brings a powerful experience of gospel truth and a personal relationship with Jesus and all those that he has placed in your life. Using biblical truths, written to open the eyes of all hearts to sins, and full of challenges by the Holy Spirit to change and grow, this is the study you need. User-friendly, even for a first time leader, it is progressive, time-sensitive, and will invite the most timid participant into heart application. I highly recommend this to all who are committed to growing closer to God and being a gospel tool to help others."

> **Nancy Puryear**, Women's ministry director (more than eleven years), Christ Community Church; cross-cultural counselor

"God used Jack Miller to help Christians, and pastors especially, to recover the gospel of Jesus Christ as the functional core of the Christian faith. Jack's famous line, 'Cheer up, you're worse off than you think,' reopened the door to many of us with an invitation to drop the pretense of a good life and to admit and delight in our continuing, desperate need for Jesus. As a church planter and trainer of church planters, I have often wished for a concise series of Bible studies that would help churches to not only know this gospel of grace, but to experience it as well. That's precisely what this series of gospel studies offers. It is a great way to biblically and relationally ground Christians in the gospel of Jesus Christ and I heartily recommend it."

> **John F. Thomas**, PhD, Director of Global Training, Redeemer City to City

"I'm probably the most "religious" person you know. I make my living teaching religious students (in seminary) to be more religious, doing religious broadcasts, writing religious books, and preaching religious sermons. It's very easy to lose the "main thing" about the Christian faith in a religious morass. These studies remind me that it's all about Jesus and Jesus is all about the Good News (the gospel). They are refreshing, informative and life changing. In fact, these studies are like a refreshing drink of cold, pure water to a thirsty man. Read and use these books from World Harvest Mission and get out of the way as you listen to the laughter and relief of the redeemed."

Steve Brown, Key Life radio broadcaster; author of *Three Free Sins: God Isn't Mad at You*

"*Gospel Growth* is unique in that it works at the very heart of our faith. It is a marriage course, a discipleship course, and a Bible study, but it is so much more. It is all about getting the central passion of Christianity–the cross of Jesus Christ–at the center of your life. And not just your thinking life, but your doing and experiencing life. So it is good theology and good practice combined. If you get the cross right, then everything else works."

Paul Miller, Director of SeeJesus (www.seeJesus.net); author of *A Praying Life*

"I've dated a lot of different curriculum in the past, but there's very little worth taking home to meet Mom. Too often, the writing is too high (too theoretical–have you actually met a sinner before?), too emotive (talk to my head and my heart!) or too clunky (really? can I accomplish this in a week–much less an evening?). WHM's new Gospel Series small group materials are rifle-ready for the foot soldier in the church to use without a lot of training, and they seem to have been written by real sinners/strugglers for fellow sinners/strugglers. Thanks, WHM, for something I can actually use!"

Geoff Bradford, Pastor, Christ the King Presbyterian Church, Raleigh, NC

GOSPEL GROWTH

BECOMING A
FAITH-FILLED PERSON

World Harvest Mission

New Growth Press
www.newgrowthpress.com

Gospel Growth: Becoming a Faith-Filled Person

New Growth Press, Greensboro, NC 27404
www.newgrowthpress.com
Copyright © 2012 by World Harvest Mission.

Gospel Growth: Becoming a Faith-Filled Person is based on portions of discipleship material developed at World Harvest Mission by Paul E. Miller which was used as the basis for *Gospel Transformation* (copyright © 2001 by World Harvest Mission) written by Neil H. Williams.

Copyright Credit for Session 7, page 68:
Mere Christianity by C. S. Lewis copyright © C. S. Lewis Pte. Ltd. 1942, 1943, 1944, 1952. Extract reprinted by permission.

Typesetting: Lisa Parnell, lparnell.com
Cover Design: Faceoutbooks, faceoutbooks.com

ISBN 978-1-936768-73-8

Printed in Canada

21 20 19 18 17 16 15 14   5 6 7 8 9

CONTENTS

INTRODUCTION

Welcome to *Gospel Growth: Becoming a Faith-Filled Person*! The gospel transforms us more into Jesus' likeness each day (2 Corinthians 3:18). This study will help you experience that more abundantly as you grow deeper in your relationship with Jesus and see how the Spirit desires to extend that growth far *beyond* you.

Gospel Growth, the second book in the "Gospel Transformation" series, focuses on the transformation of Christians by the power of the gospel. Over the course of this study we'll examine such topics as living by faith, spiritual disciplines, the role of faith and repentance in transformation, the meaning and importance of living in the power of the Spirit, the goal of sanctification in our lives, and our increasing identification with the suffering, death, and resurrection life of Christ.

As you work through *Gospel Growth*, as well as the other two books in the "Gospel Transformation" series—*Gospel Identity: Discovering Who You Really Are* and *Gospel Love: Grace, Relationships, and Everything That Gets in the Way*—you'll be encouraged to lead a life of greater faith, repentance, and love.

So, how does "gospel transformation" occur? How does it relate to life? What *are* the essentials of the Christian life, and how do they change us? That's what this series is about. Let's summarize it in four foundational points that we'll return to again and again:

1. **Cheer up! The gospel is far greater than you can imagine!** The gospel of Jesus Christ—and his power to transform our lives and relationships, communities, and ultimately, the nations—is the best news we will ever hear. It gives us a new identity, not based on race, social class, gender, theology, or a system of rules and regulations, but on faith in Jesus—and it's an identity that defines

every aspect of our lives. Because of this we no longer have to hide from our sin and pretend we have it all together. We now have a new way to live and relate to God and others every day. The good news is not only relevant to us when we first believe, but it continues to work in us and through us as we grow, visibly expressing itself in love (Galatians 5:6).

2. **Cheer up! You are worse than you think!** One of the great hindrances to Christian growth, healthy relationships, and strong communities is a life of pretense—pretending that we don't struggle with a multitude of sins, such as self-righteous attitudes, foul tempers, nagging anxieties, lustful looks, controlling and critical hearts, and a general belief that we are better than other people. Part of the good news is that God knows all this—knows *us*—already, and he wants to be the one who changes us. Because our sin blocks our intimacy with God and others, we need God's Spirit to show us our many fears and offensive ways, and we need the insights of others to encourage us and speak into our lives.

Our first two points work together in a cyclical fashion. On the one hand, none of us wants to look at our sin without knowing the good news of forgiveness and deliverance from it. On the other hand, our view of the gospel is severely limited if we do not continually see the depths of our sin. The gospel cannot soak deeply into us unless it addresses our ongoing need for it. And that brings us to the next point.

3. **Cheer up! God's Spirit works in your weakness!** We not only have a new identity, but we have been given the Spirit, who is more than sufficient to lead, guide, and empower us in our new life. The power that raised Jesus from the dead is at work in our new lives as well (Ephesians 1:19–20). Nevertheless, the power of the Spirit does not work automatically, but through repentant, obedient faith. Furthermore, this power is made evident through our weakness (2 Corinthians 12:9; 13:4). Along with Paul, we can delight in our weakness, for then we are strong and God is glorified. The result is a wonderful freedom to forget about ourselves and stop wondering whether we have enough ability—we don't.

But we can rejoice in the knowledge that God uses and empowers the weak. Therefore, we have the hope discussed in point four.

4. **Cheer up! God's kingdom is more wonderful than you can imagine!** The kingdom of God is the new and final age that began with Jesus' coming. It is the age of righteousness, peace, and joy in the Holy Spirit (Romans 14:17). The kingdom of God is about the renewing of all things, and God has made us a part of this great story of salvation. This kingdom is about the reconciliation of relationships, about the restoration of justice and equality, about freedom from every lord except Jesus, about forgiveness, and about the defeat of Satan. It is about compassion for the poor and powerless, about helping those who are marginalized and rejected by society, and about using our gifts and resources for the advancement of others. It is about new communities and the transformation of society and culture. For Paul, to preach the gospel is to preach the kingdom, and therefore to preach the whole counsel of God (Acts 20:24–27).

The goal of each study, therefore, is not simply to master the content, but to allow the gospel to master you and your group more fully. Knowledge is like bread—unless it is digested, it will go stale. The content of this course needs to be chewed, digested, and assimilated, so that true *spiritual* growth can occur. It's easy to slip into the routine of just completing the lesson, but don't. Our ultimate goal here is love—love rooted in a growing faith in Jesus, which leads to more love (Galatians 5:6).

Our prayer is that through your time together, your love for Jesus, and the people God brings into your life, you will grow deeper daily. May God bless and encourage your group as you work together through this study!

ABOUT THE SESSIONS

The sessions in this study are built to take 75 minutes apiece. They've been built so there's plenty of good content, but also plenty of room for discussion. There are suggested times for each section, but again do what you need to as a group—the goal isn't to master the content, but to allow the gospel to master you and your group.

Sessions follow a logical order, so be sure to cover them in the sequence given. Often, one session builds on what has been previously covered in the session or sessions before it. Furthermore, each session follows its own sequence so that your group can get the most impact from it. Each time you get together you can expect to see the following:

Overview—This introduction of the session includes the one point to take away from the session. Reading it as part of your group time is optional, but by stating the focus up front everyone knows what's coming.

Opening the Discussion—In this brief opening section, take time to unwind and transition from your previous environment (home, work, or some other place) and into the theme of the session. The questions here are intended to help the entire group interact. They also help set up what comes later in the session. And maybe, because you are so busy having a good time discussing a "light" question, you won't even realize you've *already* gotten down to business.

Opening the Word—This is the heart of each session, and typically the longest section. You'll spend some serious time digging into God's Word and discovering its meaning in ways you hadn't before. More importantly, you'll discover how the information you're studying applies to your life right now, and what God wants to do with it.

Opening Your Life—In this closing section you'll move from *understanding how* the Bible applies to your life to actually *applying* it. At the end of each session you will break into smaller groups or pairs to share how you will apply today's lesson and commit to following up with each other during the week. This way everyone's involved, engaged, and committed to one another. The lesson will usually give some suggestions for its application, but if God's telling you to do something else, *go for it!*

In short, in each session you'll be challenged to share, to think, and to act. And as you do, gospel transformation will be more than just the title of a Bible study series. It will be a reality you live every day.

FOR LEADERS

We strongly suggest working through each session on your own first, prior to your group time. Your prep time shouldn't require more than one-half hour, but take as much time as you need. Your goal is the same your group's—to grow in faith, repentance, and obedience. As you review the material, honestly answer each question. Ask the Spirit to reveal your own heart, and be prepared to share what the Spirit reveals with the group, as long as it's appropriate. Your own transparency and vulnerability will open the door for others.

You'll notice that there are times during the session (especially during "Opening Your Life") when we suggest getting into pairs or smaller groups. Feel free to do this at other times during the session when we haven't explicitly told you to do so. It's a great way to make sure everyone remains engaged with the material and with each other, and it frees people to share about matters they may not want to discuss with the entire group.

Also, in the back of the book are suggested answers and reflections relating to each session's questions. Don't use this section as a crutch or a shortcut. Wrestle with each question and passage on your own and as a group. Figure out its meaning for yourselves. Then, if you like, look in back to add further insight to your discussion time.

Finally, here are some expectations we encourage you to have for your group members, and to share openly with them:

1. **Expect to be challenged.** The answers will not come quickly or easily. If they do, we haven't done our job properly. As you work through each question, expect that it will take some time, thought, and soul-searching to complete each session.

2. **Expect the Holy Spirit** to be the one ultimately responsible for the growth of your group, and for the change in each person's life—including your own. Relax and trust him.

3. **Expect your group time together** to include an open, give-and-take discussion of each session's content and questions. Also expect times of prayer at each meeting. In fact, plan for them.

4. **Expect struggle.** Don't be surprised to find in your group a mixture of enthusiasm, hope, and honesty, along with indifference, anxiety, skepticism, and covering up. We are all people who need Jesus every day, so expect your group to be made up of people who wrestle with sin and have problems—just like you!

5. **Expect to be a leader** who desires to serve, but who needs Jesus as much as the rest of the group. No leader should be put on a pedestal or be expected to have the right answers. Give yourself the freedom to share openly about your own weaknesses, struggles, and sins. Covet your group's prayers.

6. **Expect confidentiality**, and be prepared to ask the group to make that commitment with you. Anything personal must be kept in confidence and never shared with others outside the group. Gossip will quickly destroy a group.

You are ready to begin. May God bless your group's journey together!

WHAT MAKES A CHRISTIAN GROW?

OVERVIEW

In this session you'll come to understand the centrality of faith in the Christian life, and to know and experience faith as the instrument for receiving the power of God.

In answering the question "What is the one thing you think you should do to grow as a Christian?" people will invariably mention the need to be more dedicated, to witness more, to read the Bible more, to pray more—in general, to *do* more things. These are not bad things! However, there is often no mention of faith and our need to develop a deepening trust in Jesus. This lesson emphasizes that faith is the instrument for receiving the power of God in our lives.

OPENING THE DISCUSSION

20 MINUTES

Leader: If this is your first time together as a group, ask everyone to introduce themselves, and to take a few moments to share what they each hope to get out of this study. (You can ask this second question even if you've been together for years.)

The sections in *italics* are for you, to help you and your group transition from one part of the session to the next. Read them verbatim, put what's here in your own words, or just move on to the next section—whatever works best for you and your group.

Since this session—this entire study, in fact—is about spiritual growth, let's take a few moments to understand what that means to each of us, and what it looks like.

Discuss the following questions:

1. What comes to mind when you hear the word *growth*? Come up with as many ideas as you can.

2. Talk about a time when you experienced a "spiritual growth spurt." What was different? Why?

Thank you for sharing about what was clearly an important time in each of your lives. In doing so, you've shown each of us that God is always at work in our lives, sometimes even when we're not aware of it. Try to keep the answers you shared (or thought) in the back of your minds—we're going to come back to them later on.

As we've also shared today, growth means different things to different people. Growth can be exciting. The results of our growth are beautiful. Growth is also uncomfortable, maybe even incredibly painful. Sometimes it's all these things at once. Spiritual growth is always an adventure, and it's an adventure that begins and ends in faith. That's why we need to allow God to take the lead, rather than thinking we somehow can make ourselves grow. So let's start the next part of that adventure together.

OPENING THE WORD

Read aloud John 6:28–29; Galatians 3:2–3, 10–14; and Hebrews 11:1–6. Then discuss these questions:

3. Based on these passages and others you can think of, how do we grow in Christ? How are your answers similar to or different from the ones you came up with in question 1?

4. Look over the following chart. What stands out to you? Why?

Believe who you are in Christ	→ Live by the Spirit	→ Become who you are in Christ
Believing effort	→ Engages the Spirit	→ Love, joy, peace
Unbelieving effort	→ Engages the flesh	→ Lust, hatred, anger

5. What makes it difficult for us to recognize when we're slipping to the bottom of this chart—in other words, when we're engaged in an unbelieving effort or trusting in things other than God?

*"Our struggle in living the Christian life
is not doing, it is believing."*
— John Owen

*"Grace is opposed to earning,
not effort."*
— Dallas Willard

6. Look at the two quotes above. How do we reconcile them? When we put both these messages together what do we learn about living by faith?

Read aloud Galatians 5:4–8; 2 Thessalonians 1:11; and 1 John 5:2–5. Then discuss the following questions:

7. How *does* faith lead to growth? What are some outward signs that spiritual growth truly is taking place within us? Give examples.

OPENING YOUR LIFE

Read Ephesians 1:13–21. Then discuss the following questions:

8. What have the Father, Son, and Spirit already done for you, based on this passage alone? Which of these things do you most wish you could know and experience more deeply right now?

We use the phrase a "leap of faith" for a reason. Picture this: A little girl is trapped upstairs in a building that's on fire. She sees her father, calling out to her to jump. But before she'll jump, what has to happen? First, she needs *the **knowledge** that her father is strong enough to catch her. She must also **believe** that it's true, and not some lie the neighbors made up. Finally, she has to **trust** that her father will catch her. Only then will she jump.*

*It's like that with us too, even after we come to Christ. Faith is clinging to, resting in, relying on, and believing in Jesus. It is the opposite of self-reliance. It is giving up on our own resources and fleeing to Christ. It is accepting who Christ is, who God is, what he has promised, and who we are in Christ. It is receiving the truths of the gospel into our lives and hearts. And as much as Christ has done for us, it's never **only** for us.*

9. Think back to the "spiritual growth spurt" we discussed in question 2. Who helped you most in taking that leap forward? What did he or she (or they) do to keep you moving forward?

10. Who do you know right now who seems ready to take the next step of faith in their lives? How can you become the person you just described for *that* person? Come up with some practical steps, if possible.

Divide into smaller groups of three or four.

*Any work we do with eternal value involves other people. Everything we do can potentially have an eternal impact on others. Think about it: how others have loved you—or failed to—is part of the reason **you** are who you are today.*

*To grow in faith, we need to exercise faith. That's why, each week, you'll get the opportunity to respond to what God wants to do in your life. Below you'll find a few options, to help you think through how to put what you've learned today into practice. Choose one of these ways to step out in faith, so that you **really** have to rely on Christ—or if God has prompted you to do something else through this session, by all means do **that**!*

*In the space that follows, write down the one thing you'll do this week to apply today's lesson to your own life. Take ten minutes to share about your choices with those in your group, and then make plans to touch base with each other before the next session, to check in and encourage one another. Your touch-base time can be face-to-face, by phone, or online, but make a commitment you can keep—and **keep** it.*

- Have you ever put into words why you believe in Jesus? Write down your testimony, your faith story in Jesus (no more than two to three pages). Then get together with a friend (Christian or not-yet Christian—it's up to you) and share what God has done in your life. Do more than just talk. Afterward, listen for opportunities to encourage and pray for your friend.

- Think of a practical way to share the blessings God has given you with someone else. It could be something as small as texting a word of encouragement to someone or cooking a meal for them, or as big as making a rent payment for a single mom who is trying to make ends meet.

- What might you do in your group to reach out to your community? Volunteer to help out at a local event? Make a special meal for your local fire department or other civic organization? Come up with a plan, and then do it!

This week I'll take a faith-filled leap by: _____

_____

_____

_____

After ten minutes, get back together and close in prayer. Pray something like this:

> *Dear God, We thank you for the relationships that are already beginning and growing in this group. We pray, as Paul does in Ephesians 1:18–19, "that the eyes of [our] heart may be enlightened in order that [we] may know the hope to which he has called [us], the riches of his glorious inheritance in the saints, and his incomparably great power for us who believe." Amen.*

WHO DO YOU SAY I AM—AND DO YOU BELIEVE IT?

2

OVERVIEW

In this session we'll discover how trusting what Jesus says about himself helps us grow in Christ.

We must always live in light of who God is, what Jesus has done, what has happened to us as a result, and the work that the Spirit is continually doing within us. Usually we define ourselves by our successes and failures, our reputation, our sin, our intelligence, beauty, and abilities (or lack of them). Moreover, we often define other people by their weaknesses, failures, and sins. Hence, we are quick to gossip and condemn others. We treat both ourselves and others like finished products. Fortunately for all of us, that's not the case.

The good news of Jesus calls us to view ourselves and other Christians very differently. Jesus defines who we are *now*. Through Jesus' work on the cross we have been declared right, forgiven, reconciled, and brought into the presence of God. We have become the dearly loved children of the living God; nothing can separate us from his love. All these truths and more are summed up in one symbol—the cross.

OPENING THE DISCUSSION

1. What are some well-known symbols or "brandings" we see in our world today—for example, a symbol of your favorite sports team or a well-known product? Come up with some examples.

2. What elements are common to these symbols? In other words, what do the creators of these symbols want you to think when you see them?

Symbols can be powerful. And often they represent a higher power—or at least convey the idea that the thing or group they represent can empower us in some ways. However, we serve—and have constant access to—a power far higher than any of the people or things we discussed. And we too have a symbol that represents that power—although it probably doesn't have a lot in common with the symbols we've just discussed. Let's come to a deeper understanding of who we are in Jesus, and the implications that has for every part of our lives.

OPENING THE WORD

Read aloud 1 Corinthians 1:18–24; Philippians 2:5–8; and Hebrews 12:1–3. Then discuss these questions together:

3. As Christians what is our symbol? What does that symbol tell us about our God, his kingdom, and the kind of life we can expect to have in Christ?

Take turns reading Mark 10:45; Romans 5:6–11, 17–19; Galatians 2:20–21; and Colossians 2:9–15. Then discuss the following questions:

4. What did Jesus accomplish on the cross? Draw out as many answers as you can from the passages you just read.

5. What does it mean for *us*, then, to be "crucified with Christ"? What are some of the implications that has for our lives?

*Jesus has done more for us than we can even hope to understand, or fully thank him for. But as we grow in Christ, we come to a deeper knowledge of what Jesus has done for us, and why he **had** to do it.*

*The "Cross chart" illustrates this point. When we become Christians, we experience an unveiling of both our sinfulness and of the holiness of God. At the same time, we see that Jesus' blood covers **all** our sin. The more we grow, the more we see our sin—and the more we see Jesus. Our need for him grows, as does our gratitude for what he's done for us.*

Review the "Cross chart." Then discuss the questions that follow.

Figure 2.1

THE CROSS CHART

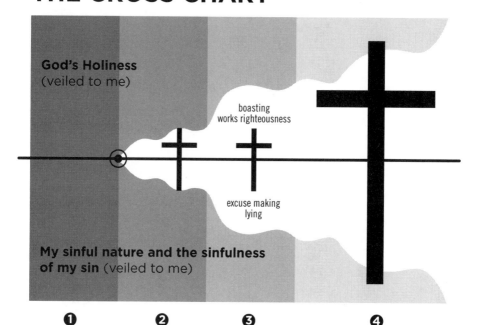

God's Holiness
(veiled to me)

boasting
works righteousness

excuse making
lying

**My sinful nature and the sinfulness
of my sin** (veiled to me)

❶	❷	❸	❹
Before Conversion	**After Conversion**	**Adjusting the Record**	**Boasting in the Cross!**
The holiness of God, my sinful nature, and the sinfulness of my sin are veiled to me	I have a limited, fluctuating, but growing awareness of both God's holiness and my sinfulness.	I resort to dishonesty and performance to bridge the gap when my belief in the gospel does not keep pace with what I know of God's holiness and my sin.	As I daily believe the gospel, the cross bridges the gap; I rest in my identity in Christ and his righteousness, which enables me to own up to God's holiness and my sinfulness without trying to adjust the record. Now, by faith, I am empowered and freed up to love God and my neighbor.

6. When have you seen evidence of each of these four steps in your life? (It's OK to use someone else's example if necessary, but use names only if it's a positive example.)

7. Look at step 3 again. In what ways do *you* try to "bridge the gap" between your knowledge of God and the degree that you actually *believe* it? What does your behavior look like in those cases?

There's another, more in-depth illustration—"How we are to live; and how we change"—that pictures our constant struggle between unbelief and faith, and where each of those paths takes us. You'll find it at the end of this session, on page 26. Our small-group time doesn't allow us to explore this illustration fully, but it's strongly recommended that you take some time to read and think through it on your own. Consider where you often are on this drawing and why, and how it's an opportunity for the Spirit to work.

Let's move on, and dig deeper into our answers to question 7.

> *"[O]nly he who believes is obedient,*
> *and only he who is obedient believes."*
> — Dietrich Bonhoeffer, *The Cost of Discipleship*

OPENING YOUR LIFE

"For every one look at your sins,
take ten looks at Christ."
— Robert Murray McCheyne

Subdivide into groups of three or four.

When our actions don't match with what we know about God, we cover our inconsistency in any number of ways—maybe even in ways we haven't realized. But often others notice it. And when they do, they call it by another name—hypocrisy.

So where is it that our actions reveal we're still not fully believing in Jesus? Let's take a closer look at our blind spots, as well as the areas where we already know we're coming up short, and allow the light of Jesus to shine into them all. Let's discover how we can believe what Jesus has done and what he has promised to do!

In the following checklist, read through God's claims and promises, as well as the reactions we often have in response to them, both positive and negative. Check off issues you most find yourself struggling to entrust to God, and try to identify the top two or three that crop up most regularly. Give yourselves up to ten minutes to work through this exercise on your own, and then discuss the questions that follow in your groups. Let's plan to come back together in twenty minutes.

God's Claims and Promises

☐ **God is in control. He saves his people (Hebrews 1:3; Jonah 2:9).**
I no longer have to manipulate people to order my world. I am not in control of my life, let alone the world. It's a good thing too, because I would make a huge mess. I cannot save my spouse, my children, or those who come to me for help. I can direct them to the One who does save. I can encourage them toward faith.

☐ **Only God can speak and it is done (Genesis 1:1–31).**
If I am God, I speak and it is done. If I try to be a godlike parent, and my will is not done, then I express my wrath just to show how god-like I really am. But I am only a creature.

☐ **God orders the world for his good, which includes using all things for my good too (Romans 8:28–29).**
I am now able rejoice in suffering because I know God is using it to make me more like him. God works through everything so that I may become more like Jesus.

☐ **He gives life and takes it away (Job 1:21).**
God owes me nothing. Everything I have comes from him. If something is taken away I have no right to fume because everything is a gift.

☐ **He is patient, kind, loving, and gracious (Jonah 4:2).**
I become like the one I worship! Am I patient, kind, loving, and gracious?

☐ **The Lord is my Shepherd (Psalm 23) and he provides (Matthew 6:26–30; 10:29; Hebrews 13:5).**
Even in the midst of people who are against me, God will help me and give me peace. He knows my needs better than I do. Look at flowers, birds, and ants to see God's wisdom, care, and provision. Do I not believe that God values me even more? How well do I rest in that knowledge?

☐ **God is all-knowing, ever-present (Psalm 139), and wise (Romans 16:27).**
I can give up pretending. I don't need to worry that God has some-how missed something important. I do not have to figure out my life. It is in God's hands. Worrying indicates that I have forgotten all this.

☐ **God is faithful (Hebrews 11; 13:8).**
God is not going to abandon me. He will persevere with me. His faithfulness is grounded in his character, not in my obedience or lack thereof. Look at other believers, past and present. Why would God not care for me as much as he has for them?

☐ **God is my Father (Hebrews 12:5–12).**
I now accept hardship as loving discipline, not as something "God has to fix." I trust God to provide for me. He loves me.

☐ **God is good, truthful, and just (Deuteronomy 32:4; Hebrews 6:18).**
I can trust everything he says and does to be right and good. There is no need, or reason, for me to distrust him.

☐ **God is the divine warrior (Exodus 15).**
I do not have to take revenge when I have been hurt or wronged.
God fights for me.

☐ **God is humble (Isaiah 6; 57:15).**
He opposes the proud and their message, so I don't have to. I do not
have to fight pride with pride. God lives with the humble.

☐ **When I look at the heavens, what are human beings (Psalm 8:3–4)?**
Who are people anyway? The sun came up today without anyone's
help. Isn't God more powerful than any circumstance I face today?

☐ **God says, "Never will I leave you" (Hebrews 13:5).**
Note that this promise is given in the context of the love of money. It
is given to specifically address a particular idol. Believing this promise frees me to stop loving money and trusting in it for my security.

☐ **God will make a new heaven and earth. There will be no more tears,
crying, or sorrow (2 Peter 3:13; Revelation 21:4).**
My home is not here. My true hope is not in this present world. My
citizenship is in heaven. Jesus has prepared a place elsewhere for me.
One day everything will be put right. This comforts me in suffering
and grief. I do not mourn as those without hope.

☐ **I have an unfading inheritance in Christ (1 Peter 1:4).**
Everything I own now will end up in the trash heap sooner or later.
Where is my treasure?

☐ **I won't be tempted beyond what I can bear (1 Corinthians 10:13).**
When I am feeling hopeless or overwhelmed, I need to believe this
promise and receive its truth into my heart. My temptation is *not*
beyond what I can bear.

☐ **"Whoever acknowledges me before men, I will also acknowledge
before my Father in heaven" (Matthew 10:32).**
This promise encourages me to share the gospel with others. How
am I responding to that encouragement, and the promise that comes
with it?

☐ **Rejoice! All these promises are mine because I am united to Christ.
"For no matter how many promises God has made, they are 'Yes' in
Christ" (2 Corinthians 1:20).**
Full salvation, glorification, abundant life, holiness, redemption, and
every blessing are mine in Christ (Ephesians 1:3). Do I truly *believe*
it?

8. Which of God's claims and promises do you find yourself most strug-gling with? Were there any not mentioned here?

9. On the other hand, as you reviewed this list, when did you find your-self thinking, Yes, Jesus *has* dealt with that one in my life—that one *has* been getting crucified with Christ? How did Jesus bridge the gap that you couldn't?

10. Now, look again at those two or three items that crop up most, and the promises connected with them. How will remembering Jesus' faith-fulness to you help you allow him to address *those* items? What might that look like?

Leader: After twenty minutes, regain everyone's attention, keeping them with their groups. Ask for volunteers from each group to share insights from their discussion time.

---

*Think about your answers to the last couple of questions. Rather than give you additional choices, let's consider our answers as God's challenge to us this week. Share those answers with your group if you haven't already. Then take a few minutes to pray for **God's** answers to those questions.*

When you're done praying, stay quiet or move into another room, to give other groups a chance to share and pray together. Also, set a time to touch base before the next session, to encourage and continue praying for each another. In the space that follows, write down what you're doing in response to this week's session. May God help each of you walk deeper in belief this week!

This week, I'll live out my belief in Christ: _____

_____

_____

_____

The diagram below provides an overview of the Christian life: how we are to live and how we change. Suffering does not automatically harden or soften our hearts. The same fire that hardens the clay can melt the wax. It all depends on our response.

Blocks 1–4 show the progress of unbelief. Our unbelief and lack of repentance engages the flesh, which then expresses itself sinfully—in gossip, anger, lust, and so on, (block 4). This, in turn, adds to our experience of suffering and temptation in this world. We have now compounded our difficulties.

Block 5 (faith) is the other route we can take. This block is in direct contrast to block 1 (unbelief).

Blocks 6–8 show how faith and repentance engage the Spirit, who wages war against the flesh and expresses himself through love. This in turn impacts our world for good.

Figure 2.2

How the Gospel Transforms Us

Refuse → Resist → Rant and Rave

1 **Unbelief**
- Subterranean Sin
- Idolatry
- Evil Desires

2 **Worldly Sorrow**
- False repentance
- No repentance

3 The Flesh

4 **Surface Sin**
- Sin that can be videotaped (with sound!)
- Lack of love

WAR
Galatians 5:17

5 **Faith**
Believing what God says
- Who we are in Christ
- Who God is
- His Promises

6 **Repentance**
- Owning up to the flesh
- Repenting of idolatry, surface sin, and worldly sorrow

7 Spirit

8 **Obedience**
- Fruit of the Spirit
- Love

Receive → Repent → Run

WASTING TIME WITH GOD

OVERVIEW

In this session you'll explore how to develop intimacy with God through spiritual disciplines such as prayer, Bible study, and worship.

The spiritual disciplines are both a wonderful grace given us by God and an often-misunderstood activity. If we're honest, sometimes they can feel like "one more thing" we're supposed to do to be good Christians. We may even unconsciously begin to think of them as something "we have to do or God will be upset with us," which eventually makes our prayer life into little more than an attempt to manipulate God to either get our way or avoid being punished. We do far better to come to God with sensitive and repentant hearts, knowing his love for us doesn't depend on how long or how often we have our quiet times.

Spiritual disciplines don't make us grow—that's the Holy Spirit's job. However, the disciplines—or better yet, "intimacy-building practices"— put us in a place and posture where we can most readily hear the Father's love for us anew each day. Likewise, the disciplines aren't just "things we do to connect to God." More importantly, they're an expression of the grace God has already given us—and an expression of the desire to go deeper into the restored relationship we now have with God. In a sense, through intimacy-building practices such as Bible study, prayer and worship, we preach God's goodness and truth to ourselves, even when we are unable to feel it. We know our hearts grow cold all too easily. But by dedicating time to focus on God's presence, we also acknowledge our desire to truly know God better and to allow him to transform our hearts. From this position of weakness, God makes us truly strong in Christ.

OPENING THE DISCUSSION

15 MINUTES

Discuss the following questions:

1. What activity do you most enjoy doing with a friend?

2. How does doing that activity together show the other person that he or she is important to you? How does it help *you* enjoy that activity more?

3. What activity do you most enjoy doing with *God*?

Today we're going to explore how we can respond to, enjoy, and be-come more connected with God through the spiritual disciplines. These intimacy-building activities include prayer, Bible study, and worship. To many people, even many Christians, it seems that we really ought to get *up and **do** something, instead of "**just** pray" or "**just** read the Bible." But what's more important than being in God's presence?*

*In a sense, all the disciplines are forms of worship—ways to acknowledge that we serve a great God, to recognize God's "worth-ship," and to draw closer to him. They get us out of our own way so we can see and appreciate God for who **he** is. By engaging in these practices, we declare that God is God—and we aren't. And thank God for **that**! So let's discover some of the ways we can "waste time with God."*

"But you might wish to think about . . . whether you really would be comfortable for eternity in the presence of One whose company you have not found especially desirable for the few hours and days of your earthly existence."
— Dallas Willard, *The Great Omission*

OPENING THE WORD

Read John 15:1–8 and Luke 10:38–42. Then discuss the following questions:

4. Why is it so important to remain in Jesus—to just spend time with him, speaking with him, listening to him? Why is it better than simply doing things for him?

5. How has your relationship with Jesus—and your ways of relating to him—changed over the course of your Christian life?

6. Talk about a meaningful time or season of worship, prayer, or Bible study you've had in the past. What made it so meaningful to you?

The disciplines are a practical way of getting our eyes off ourselves and onto God, making relationship with him the center of our lives. However, it's still more than possible to make times of prayer, Bible study, worship, or other disciplines about us. Let's look at a couple biblical examples of that.

Read John 5:39–40; Matthew 6:7, 16–18; and Luke 11:42. Then discuss the following questions:

7. Where do you see a disconnect between what God desired and what each of these "practitioners of spiritual disciplines" did? Why do you think this disconnect occurred?

8. We don't like to think of ourselves as Pharisees. Nonetheless, how have you been guilty of these practices and/or attitudes? When have you allowed your time with God to become stale and lifeless?

9. On the other hand, when have those dry periods led to a fresh connection with God, in a way other than what you'd become accustomed to?

10. How do those experiences speak to the fact we're in a *relationship* with God—one that deepens with intimacy over time and requires us to remain sensitive to the changes in that relationship?

OPENING YOUR LIFE

"More things are wrought by prayer,
than this world dreams of."
— Alfred Lord Tennyson

In the spirit of our last question, we're going to wrap up our time together a little differently today. We're going to spend some time meditating on the Lord's Prayer, which serves as the pattern and foundation of our prayers. To help us connect with this prayer and make it our own, we'll follow an ancient practice called lectio divina, *or the "spiritual reading" of the text. If you enjoy this activity and find it meaningful, you can learn more about it after this session, on pages 35–36.*

Leader: Ask everyone to get comfortable; if people want to sit on the floor or lay down on the furniture in your meeting area, let them. Also consider dimming the lights during this time. Once everyone's comfortable, ask them to close their eyes, take a few deep breaths, and spend a couple of minutes in silence, quieting their hearts and removing distracting thoughts.

Let the group know you will read through the Lord's Prayer aloud twice (Matthew 6:9–13, printed below), and afterward you'll provide direction to help them process—but that they should remain silent. Encourage everyone to listen for what God may be saying to them through this activity.

Read Matthew 6:9–13 aloud, slowly. After your first reading, let the silence hang for about a half-minute. Then read it again, slowly.

> Our Father in heaven, hallowed be your name, your kingdom come, your will be done on earth as it is in heaven. Give us today our daily bread. And forgive us our debts,

as we also have forgiven our debtors. And lead us not into temptation, but deliver us from the evil one.

Continue with the following exercise. (Comments in parentheses are for leaders only.)

- What word, phrase, or theme stood out to you as you listened to this prayer? *(Give everyone about fifteen seconds to focus. Again, make sure everyone remains silent.)*

- Take a minute to meditate or ponder on that word, phrase, or theme. How is it speaking to you and where you're at right now? What do you think God may be trying to tell you? *(Give group members a minute to meditate.)*

- For the next three minutes, silently have an honest conversation with your Father. Tell him what's on your heart; dialogue silently about what God appears to be bringing up, and ask God what he wants you to do about it. Try to allow time to listen for God's answer. *(Allow three minutes for people to silently pray. Quietly give them a heads-up when there's a minute remaining.)*

Turn to a partner and take up to ten minutes to quietly share how God spoke to you during this time of prayer, and how you believe God wants you to respond. If this activity didn't resonate with you and/or you don't know how to respond, that's okay—choose from one of the challenges below. Also, make plans to touch base with each other before the next session. In the space that follows, write down what you're doing in response to this week's session.

- What's one way God might be calling you to change your relationship with him right now? Perhaps our *lectio divina* activity has inspired you to try it as a regular practice—see pages 35–36 for more details. Or maybe your worship time needs to be something that doesn't only happen in church. Or maybe you need to make regular time to be quiet before the Lord and just *listen*. Whatever it is, begin putting it into practice this week, and see where God takes you.

- Want to go deeper into the Bible, prayer, and worship? Spend some time in the Psalms this week. At the very least, try Psalms 1; 19; 23; 40—41; 50—51; 104; 130—131; 136; 139; and 144—150. And don't just read—*meditate*—on these psalms; consider everything God (and the psalmist) is saying. As you complete each psalm, thank God for who he is, and let these psalms be a spur to worshiping God more deeply.

- As we've discussed, it can become easy to go through the motions in our devotional time. Consciously commit to not letting that happen this week. As you start, be quiet before God. Picture God in all his glory. Desire to encounter and worship God with a sense of reverence, awe, and devotion. Reflect on how this affects not only the times when you're specifically focused on God but other parts of your life.

This week, I'll grow in my relationship with God by: _____

_____

_____

_____

After ten minutes, close this session in prayer, asking God to help you all live out what he's shown, and to help you grow in grace and intimacy as you pursue your relationships with him and enjoy his presence.

Practicing Lectio Divina

The standard form of *lectio divina* dates back to the twelfth century, although the practice is much older. It is *slowly* approaching the biblical text in a way that helps us really *hear* what it's saying, to *personalize* the text to our unique situations, to respond to God in *prayer*, and to *live* out the text. Many times we simply read too fast and superficially; we need to slow down. *Lectio divina* can be compared to enjoying a nourishing three-course meal at your favorite restaurant instead of a speeding through a meal at a fast-food joint.

First we will explain this method, and then you will have an opportunity to try it. This exercise may be done individually or in a group. There are four main parts to this way of approaching Scripture.

1. *Lectio:* **the slow reading of the text.** As you approach the text, take time to read aloud or to yourself, and treat the text as a letter directly written to you. Reflect on what you have read and don't rush. Listen to the gentle whisper of God speaking to you (1 Kings 19:12). Read through it two or three times, spending some time in silence between readings. Read until you find a particular word, phrase, or theme that speaks to you and captures your attention. This could be a word of comfort *or* disruption.

2. *Meditatio:* **meditating on the text.** Here you focus on the particular words, phrase, or theme that stood out in your reading. This meditating is pondering or ruminating on one particular part of the text. Repeat to yourself the piece of text, and even memorize it. As you meditate on it, how does it speak to you—to your hopes, fears, or desires? What thoughts or memories come to mind? What is God saying to you this moment, on this day? What is God telling you about himself, about yourself, about your situation, or about people you know?

3. *Oratio:* **praying the text.** The text now forms the basis for a conversation with your Father. Talk to him about what's on your heart and what your meditation has brought to

your attention. Your prayer is now your response to God and may include thanks, questions, frustrations, praise, requests, or confession of sin.

4. *Contemplatio:* **putting the text into practice.** Although this word sounds like doing nothing, this step emphasizes putting the text into action—living the text. This may be described as restful activity! It is living before God and enjoying his presence. Here you take what you have read, meditated on, prayed, and go and live it. This is the full reception of the text, the incarnation of the text in your life—living it before God.

As a biblical example, consider Mary's interaction with the word of God in Luke 1:26–38:

Lectio: The word of God comes to Mary through the angel Gabriel, "Greetings, you who are highly favored! The Lord is with you" (Luke 1:28). The word is personal and direct to Mary. Mary is in a position to hear the word of God.

Meditatio: Mary considers the word to her, "Mary was greatly troubled at his words and wondered what kind of greeting this might be" (Luke 1:29). She ponders on the word and what it might mean.

Oratio: She responds, "How will this be…since I am a virgin?" (Luke 1:34). Mary enters into a dialogue with God, sharing the questions that are on her heart.

Contemplatio: Mary lives the word by replying, "I am the Lord's servant….May it be to me as you have said" (Luke 1:38). The Word becomes incarnate as Mary lives out what God says to her. She allows the word of God to live in her richly (Colossians 3:16).

May you have a taste of Mary's experience as you let the Word of God live in you richly!

BUT ARE YOU *REALLY* SORRY?

4

OVERVIEW

In this session we'll discover what true repentance is, and how it differs from the false forms of repentance we often let ourselves get away with.

Relationships—with God and with others—mean saying you're sorry, *and meaning it.* The problem is, false repentance and genuine repentance can look very much alike on the surface. But beneath the surface, there's a world of difference. In this session we'll examine both worlds.

On the surface, it appears as though the Israelites (Micah 6:6–8), Saul (1 Samuel 15:24–31), and Judas (Matthew 27:3–5) are sincerely repentant. However, as we will see, even though they are aware of their sinfulness, their hearts are far from God. We'll also examine two examples of genuine repentance: David and the prodigal son. Using these examples, we'll draw out various aspects of genuine repentance.

From there, we'll turn our focus to how we relate with others—both believer and unbeliever—and where we need to seek to repent and mean it. Where genuine repentance occurs, healing occurs as well—for us and for those from whom we truly seek forgiveness. And where healing occurs, so does growth.

OPENING THE DISCUSSION

10 MINUTES

1. What's the worst excuse anyone's ever given you for their behavior? Use a humorous example, and provide a little background behind the incident.

The examples we just shared might have given us a few good laughs, but the excuses we give for our behavior aren't always funny. In fact, excuses can be tragic, especially when they involve behavior we should regret and repent from doing. Our attempts to downplay or excuse our wrong behavior—presented without any real intention of changing—show a disregard for others and often hurt them deeply. It exposes our own insincerity and selfishness—which often is a much bigger wrong than the one we're trying to excuse away. Most of all, it offends God.

*True repentance goes far deeper than apologizing for bad behavior. It's an acknowledgment that, deep down, we are much worse than our behavior. It's also more than just admitting that we're wrong—it's confessing that we truly **want** to be better than we know we are. It's asking God to turn us around because we know we can't do it on our own. Repentance isn't just an action—it's a way of life and a necessary part of our ongoing relationship with Christ. It is a turning from our self-sufficiency and self-preoccupation, which in turn, allows us to become more dependent on Jesus alone. As we trust in the work of Jesus and in the power of the Spirit, we become more honest and transparent toward others, and that allows them to see God's grace working within us.*

Today we'll examine biblical examples of both false and genuine repentance and begin to discover together how repentance opens us up to the deeper work God wants to do in our lives.

"True repentance is the return to God with which the Christian life begins, continues, and ends."
— Sinclair Ferguson

OPENING THE WORD

40 MINUTES

Divide into subgroups of three or four. Read one of the following Scripture passages.

- Micah 6:1–8

- 1 Samuel 15:1–3, 7–31

- Matthew 26:23–25, 47–50; 27:3–5

Leader: If there are more than three subgroups have more than one group read the same passage.

Take fifteen minutes to read and then discuss the following questions:

2. What specific sins are committed in this passage?

3. What kind of repentance and/or obedience is God specifically looking for?

4. What do the people in these passages do instead "to make up for" their sin, as a "substitute repentance"? What is God's response (if it's in the passage—and if not, what do you *think* God's response would be)?

Bring everyone back together after 15 minutes. Ask a representative from each group to share answers and insights from the passage they studied. Then discuss the following questions together:

5. In your own words, what are the people in your passages saying to God with their actions—by repenting their way instead of God's way?

6. When have you substituted for genuine repentance doing something to "make up for it"? Share as much as you're comfortable.

The people of the Bible were no strangers to false repentance—and by our own admission, neither are we. But the Bible also provides positive examples of true repentance. Let's look at one of them.

Read 2 Samuel 12 and Psalm 51. Then discuss the following questions:

7. In what ways does David fully realize and acknowledge his sin in these passages? What forms of false repentance could he have presented to Nathan?

8. How did David's repentance lead to the kind of works that please God? How do those actions differ from simply making up for it?

Looking at David's example, we might come away with the impression that we only need to repent when we've done something "big." However, we commit sins that need to be repented of every day. As we're called to live by faith, we are also called to live by repentance. Repentance is not something we do just once at conversion; it is a mark of the ongoing Christian life. We'll explore this more in our next session, but let's begin that exploration today.

> *"When our Lord and Master, Jesus Christ, said 'repent,' he meant that the entire life of believers should be one of repentance."*
> — Martin Luther

OPENING YOUR LIFE

Read Luke 15:11–32 and discuss the following questions:

9. What evidence do you see here that the younger son's repentance was genuine? That it wasn't? What's the father's response, regardless?

10. Do we *have* to get repentance "just right" before it's acceptable to God? How is a genuine, but imperfect, repentance different from a false repentance? Give examples.

Divide again into subgroups.

*We're all in process, but we have to be willing to **be part** of that process. Recognizing how unrepentant our hearts are is a big first step. The chart below breaks down our attitudes even further, contrasting shallow repentance with deepening repentance, and worldly sorrow with the godly sorrow that leads to true repentance. In your groups, take ten minutes to review the chart and discuss the questions that follow.*

Afterward, take five more minutes to review this week's challenges and share which one you will take on. Again, if God has prompted you to do something else through this session, do that instead. Also make plans to touch base with each other before the next session. We'll close together in prayer in fifteen minutes.

Shallow Repentance	Deepening Repentance
Shallow repentance is our usual way of saying "I'm sorry." It rarely costs us much pain.	*Deepening repentance reflects the lifestyle that Jesus calls us to. It will often cost us some pain, because we need to die to self.*
I'm only sorry for what I DO.	I'm sorry also for what I AM.
I confess after I have sinned.	I'm continually repentant because of my sin.
I focus on my behavior and desire moral reformation.	I focus on my disposition and desire spiritual transformation.
I want quick resolution so that you will get off my back.	I want deeper insight, so I need you to hang in there with me.
I can't believe I'm like that. Let's not talk about it anymore.	I can't believe I'm like that. We need to talk about it more.
I have an explanation.	I am sick of my explanations.
I repent by trying to do it right next time.	I repent that I don't have my own righteousness, and trust Christ to be my righteousness.
I'm sorry because I got found out.	I'm thankful that you brought this to my attention.
I'm sorry I offended you.	I'm sorrowful that my sinful heart is so offensive.
I feel guilty for not more actively sharing my faith.	My heart is broken when my unbelief keeps me from sharing my faith with those who don't yet know Jesus.
I know I need to do more to show the love of Jesus to others; I feel bad just doing nothing.	The Spirit is convicting me to reach out and talk with others about Christ. I can see how my current need for Jesus is the same as theirs.

11. What insights do you have as you look over this chart? Which examples of "shallow repentance" resonate most with you, and why?

12. Think about your last answer again, and the example of "deepening repentance" that corresponds with it. How might listening to others we've offended, with *that* attitude of humility, help our repentance to be more complete? (If you have extra time, consider role-playing your situations with one another.)

This week's challenges:

- Where are you struggling with repentance right now? Who do you need to share that with? Is it someone who doesn't know Jesus, whom your apology could open a door with? Is it someone who can help keep you accountable? Whoever it is, make time with him or her this week. Say what you need to say, but spend more time listening.

- Try practicing a deeper repentance with someone who doesn't know Jesus, and pay attention to what God does with it. If that person asks about your change of heart and behavior, share what

God's been doing in your heart to make that change possible. If God's given you insights from today's session you think would be helpful, be sure to share those as well.

- Is there a David you need to be a Nathan to? Set aside a time to sit down with that person. Pray for God's wisdom, that your words come out in such a way that they bring repentance and healing rather than defensiveness and anger—and that if the latter happen anyway, that you can model God's grace in the midst of it.

This week because I'm not just sorry about what I've done but need God to change who I *am*, I'll: _____

_____

_____

_____

After fifteen minutes, get back together and close in prayer. Pray something like the following:

> *Dear God, We ask that you would reveal to us those areas where we settle for worldly sorrow instead of godly sorrow. We pray that you would bring about a spirit of true repentance in each person's life. Please keep our spirits tender, so that we are able to learn and maintain a lifestyle of repentance before you Lord. Amen.*

STARTING OVER— GOD'S WAY

OVERVIEW

In this session we'll look more deeply into the lifelong connection between repentance and transformation, and we will learn how to more strongly establish that connection in our lives.

As we began to explore in our last session, repentance is not something we do just once; it is an ongoing process throughout the Christian life. Repentance is not just turning back—more importantly, it is starting over. And the hard but good news is that if we're living faith-filled lives, we will *always* be beginners, "being transformed into his likeness with ever-increasing glory" (2 Corinthians 3:18).

In a faith-filled heart, repentance breeds growth. Growth breeds room for God to reveal hidden sin as we are ready to deal with it. The revelation of deeper sin breeds deeper repentance in a faith-filled heart. And deeper repentance breeds deeper growth. And so the process starts all over.

But there's also an attitude that goes with this ongoing action of repentance, and that's where we will spend most of our time today. This session centers on the theme, "God gives grace to the humble." We'll further cement the relationship between repentance and God's transforming work in our lives, and in so doing come to know and experience the many blessings that come to us through humility.

OPENING THE DISCUSSION

In our last session, we began to touch on the connection between repentance and humility. Let's begin today by focusing more on the humility end of things.

1. Think about a humbling situation you've faced—for example, a layoff or demotion at work, something big you tried that failed in front of everyone, or even something embarrassing that happened when you were growing up. Besides "humbled" or "humiliated," how else would you describe your feelings when this event took place?

2. What good, if any, do you think came out of that situation?

*Thank you for opening up to each other. You just risked further humbling and took a chance anyway—congratulations! In order to lead a lifestyle of repentance, we need a **lot** of humility. The good news is that God hasn't left us to solve this issue alone. We have both the example of Christ and the conviction of the Spirit to help guide us. And there are many other examples from Scripture to assure us that we're on the right track. Let's begin exploring those.*

OPENING THE WORD

Take turns reading the following passages. After each one, stop and identify at least one result, fruit, benefit, or blessing that comes from repentance or humility. Record group answers on a whiteboard or pad.

a. "He who conceals his sins does not prosper, but whoever confesses and renounces them finds mercy." (Proverbs 28:13)

b. "This is what the Sovereign LORD, the Holy One of Israel, says: 'In repentance and rest is your salvation, in quietness and trust is your strength, but you would have none of it.'" (Isaiah 30:15)

c. "For this is what the high and lofty One says—he who lives forever, whose name is holy: 'I live in a high and holy place, but also with him who is contrite and lowly in spirit, to revive the spirit of the lowly and to revive the heart of the contrite.'" (Isaiah 57:15)

d. "Therefore this is what the LORD says: 'If you repent, I will restore you that you may serve me.'" (Jeremiah 15:19)

e. "Produce fruit in keeping with repentance." (Matthew 3:8)

f. "Therefore, whoever humbles himself like this child is the greatest in the kingdom of heaven." (Matthew 18:4)

g. "Peter replied, 'Repent and be baptized, every one of you, in the name of Jesus Christ for the forgiveness of your sins. And you will receive the gift of the Holy Spirit.'" (Acts 2:38)

h. "Repent, then, and turn to God, so that your sins may be wiped out, that times of refreshing may come from the Lord." (Acts 3:19)

i. "When they heard this, they had no further objections and praised God, saying, 'So then, God has granted even the Gentiles repentance unto life.'" (Acts 11:18)

j. "Godly sorrow brings repentance that leads to salvation and leaves no regret." (2 Corinthians 7:10)

k. "Those who oppose him he must gently instruct, in the hope that God will grant them repentance leading them to a knowledge of the truth, and that they will come to their senses and escape from the trap of the devil, who has taken them captive to do his will." (2 Timothy 2:25–26)

l. "Young men, in the same way be submissive to those who are older. All of you, clothe yourselves with humility toward one another, because, 'God opposes the proud but shows favor to the humble.' Humble yourselves, therefore, under God's mighty hand, that he may lift you up in due time." (1 Peter 5:5–6)

m. "If we confess our sins, he is faithful and just and will forgive us our sins and purify us from all unrighteousness." (1 John 1:9)

n. "Remember the height from which you have fallen! Repent and do the things you did at first." (Revelation 2:5)

Review your list of answers, and then discuss the following:

3. If all of these benefits belong to us when we humbly repent before God, why are we so reluctant to do it?

Take a minute to review the illustration "Repentance and humility," which contains many of the fruits and benefits of repentance we just discussed. Then let's continue our discussion.

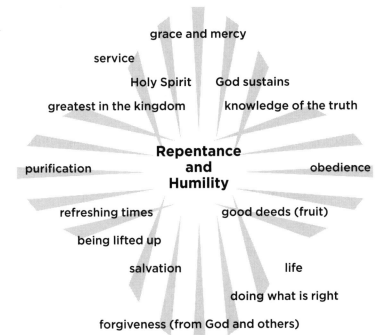

Figure 5.1: Repentance and Humility   © 2006 World Harvest Mission

4. What insights have you gotten about repentance, after studying the verses and the "Repentance and humility" illustration? How would you describe the role of repentance in transformation?

*"[T]he purpose of repentance is
to repeatedly tap into the joy of our union
with Christ in order to weaken our need
to do anything contrary to God's heart."*
— Tim Keller

Read Romans 12:1–5 and Colossians 2:18–23. Then discuss the following questions:

5. What's the connection between humility and transformation, according to these passages? What does false humility look like?

6. What does it mean to be a "living sacrifice" (Romans 12:1), both in terms of our relationship with God and our relationships with others? Give examples of each.

7. Think again about all you've learned today concerning repentance *and* faith. Why are the two inseparable? Why does one, of necessity, include the other?

If change is only in our heads, it's a short-lived change at best. But when we lay down our pride and become willing to allow God to change us, he takes over and it happens. Our hearts and spirits change, and our bodies (and heads) follow. Our "sacrifice" becomes something we do joyfully instead of grudgingly. Our desire to put ourselves above others drops. Instead, we want them to experience the same joy we have experienced. Let's explore this even further.

OPENING YOUR LIFE

Humility, repentance, and faith all work together—in us, and in those God leads us to serve. In fact, the places where God allows us to be broken are often the places God calls us to serve out of. Brokenness and beauty, sorrow and joy are all intimately connected.

Review the table, "Brokenness and beauty," taking time to think through each row, and then discuss the questions that follow.

Figure 5.2

Brokenness and beauty

	brokenness	beauty
Two Cries	What a wretched person I am! (Romans 7:24)	Thanks be to God for Jesus (Romans 7:25)
Two "Cheer Ups"	Cheer up! You're worse than you think!	Cheer up! Jesus is greater than you think!
Two Realities	I am the chief of sinners. I have unclean lips (Isaiah 6:5). I owe 10,000 bags of gold (Matthew 18:24).	I am a saint, holy, dearly loved. My sins are atoned for (Isaiah 6:7). I am forgiven (Matthew 18:27).
Two Feet	Repentance	Faith
Two Messages	"Bad" News	Good News
Two Calls	Come and die (Mark 8:34).	Come and dine (Isaiah 55:1–2).

© 2006 World Harvest Mission

8. As you review "Brokenness and beauty," what connections between brokenness and beauty strike you? What other connections come to mind?

9. How do these connections free us to be more transparent about our shortcomings, as well as reach out to others in their shortcomings? How are we and the people we reach out to enabled to lead lifestyles of repentance?

Have group members get into pairs.

Take ten minutes to review this week's challenges, and share which one you'll take on—or whether you'll take on something else God has prompted you to do instead. Close your time together in prayer. When you're done, stay quiet or move into another room, to give other pairs a chance to share and pray together. Also make plans to touch base with each other before the next session. Write what you're doing in response to this week's session in the space below. May God help each of you to walk deeper in the beauty of brokenness this week!

- Where have your points of repentance been? When have you experienced God's deep forgiveness in your life? Who's going through a similar situation whom Jesus could help right now? (Hint: He or she doesn't need to be a Christian.) Make time to meet with that person. Share how God has brought beauty out of brokenness in your life. Spend time in prayer, and if the other person's willing, commit to a season of getting together to encourage and pray for that person in his or her struggles.

- In what specific ways is humility still difficult for you? Spend an extended time with God this week dealing with it. If possible, make it a time of fasting as well. Humble yourself before God, pouring out those areas you still struggle with, and allow him to be the one to lift you up (James 4:10).

- Where is God calling you to be a "living sacrifice" now? What is God calling you to give up—an attitude, an action, a material possession, a focus on self that blinds you toward to the needs of those who don't yet know Jesus? Commit to giving that sacrifice to God this week, and beyond.

This week I'll take a faith-filled step of repentance by: _____

_____

_____

_____

6

WHO IS
THE SPIRIT,
AND WHAT DOES
HE WANT?

OVERVIEW

In this session we'll discover more about the role of the Holy Spirit in our lives and the desires he has for us.

As we've already discovered, we encounter many obstacles on the road to transformation. We struggle with sins that have become ingrown habits; we have a persistent, self-centered flesh; and we are attacked by the world and the devil. We all want to change, to stop doing wrong, and to become more loving. The million-dollar question is, "How can we change?" Clearly, we need power outside of ourselves.

In our last two sessions, we looked at faith and repentance—instruments of growth that are our responses to Christ's love and sacrifice on our behalf. Now, for the next few weeks, we'll go beyond ourselves and turn our focus to the work of the Spirit. We don't simply want to know the work of the Spirit, but grow in our personal knowledge of what the Spirit wants to accomplish in our lives. As we learn the role and desires of the Spirit, we'll more deeply understand that the Spirit does only works in *our* lives, but by doing so can work in *every* life God puts in our path.

OPENING THE DISCUSSION

10 MINUTES

1. Think of a time you took a friend or relative for granted. What happened? How did it *get* to the point where you weren't giving that person the attention he or she deserved?

*We're all guilty of having taken those we care about for granted at one time or another. As we've learned throughout this study, in our pursuit of things other than God, we tend to take God for granted as well, placing ourselves and our "needs" above him. When we do this it is ultimately at the cost (or at least deferral) of our own joy, our growth, and the good works God has planned for us in advance (Ephesians 2:10). Even within the Trinity, however, there's one member we tend to take for granted. We honor the Father; we're grateful for the atoning work of the Son; but what about the Spirit—the one whom Jesus himself promised would live **within us** (John 14:17)?*

Over the next few sessions, we'll examine the role of the Spirit in our growth, the desires the Spirit has for us, the power the Spirit gives us, and the fruit we can expect to produce by living a Spirit-filled life. In this session we'll focus specifically on knowing the Spirit better so we can better understand when it's the Spirit who's leading and when it's "just us." So let's get started.

OPENING THE WORD

Take turns reading the passages below, and then discuss the questions that follow.

- John 14:25–27

- John 16:7–15

- Acts 1:4–8

- Romans 8:9–16

- Romans 8:26–27

- 1 Corinthians 2:9–15

- 2 Corinthians 3:7–9, 16–18

- Galatians 4:6–7

- Ephesians 1:13–14

2. Based on these passages and others you're aware of, how would you explain to a friend who has no familiarity with Christianity who the Holy Spirit is and what the Spirit does? (Take your time on this question.)

3. What's the Spirit trying to *do*, specifically, in these passages? In other words, what does it look like when it's the Spirit who's guiding us? What pleases the Spirit? Explain.

4. Out of the attributes of the Spirit we've just read about, which ones have you clearly seen at work in your life? Share a little about what that's looked like.

5. On the other hand, which ideas here about the Spirit are new to you, or still difficult to fully understand? Explain.

Now that we have a better understanding of who the Spirit is, let's circle back to how we take the Spirit for granted—and how we try to do "spiritual" things without the Spirit.

Read aloud the quote from Richard Lovelace below. Also read Galatians 3:2–5. Then discuss the following questions:

> *"Most congregations of professing Christians today are saturated with a kind of dead goodness, an ethical respectability which has its motivational roots in the flesh rather than in the . . . Holy Spirit."*
> — Richard F. Lovelace, *Dynamics of Spiritual Life*

6. When have you seen this situation occur among "congregations of professing Christians"? (Avoid naming names as you discuss.) Why do you think it happens?

7. How do *you* take—or how have you taken—things out of the Spirit's hands in your own life? Why do you think you've done it?

8. Now let's look at the positive side. When was there a time in your life that you can now look back and say, "The Spirit *had* to have been in that"? Share a little bit about it. How did that experience grow your faith?

OPENING YOUR LIFE

Read Luke 4:1–2, 14–21 and Acts 16:6–10. Then discuss the following questions:

9. What strikes you about these passages? How are you encouraged by the incidents described here?

10. How can other people help us understand how (or when) the Spirit's trying to guide us? On the other hand, how can others get in the way of us hearing what the Spirit's *trying* to tell us?

11. How we can train our "spiritual ears" so we really know when it's the Spirit who's trying to guide us? What would that look like in your life, specifically?

Have everyone get into pairs.

How can you reach beyond yourself and depend on the Spirit even more? The challenges below will help you do that. Take ten minutes to review them and share which one you'll take on—or whether you'll take on something else the Spirit's guiding you to do instead. Also make plans to touch base with each other before the next session. Write what you're doing in response to this week's session in the space below.

- Think about how your life has already been transformed through the work of the Spirit. How can you share that with someone? What might that kind of transformation look like in *that* person's life? Commit to calling that person this week and setting up a time to meet.

- Go out for coffee or pizza with friends this week. Are they struggling with issues the Spirit could help them with? Have they even *considered* turning to God for help? Read Romans 8:6–11 and challenge them to take God at his word. Share how the work of the Spirit has made a difference in your life. Share something from this session, if it will help. The point is to get your friends to start asking themselves the important questions and open themselves to the answers the Spirit desires to give them.

- Who are the powerless in your community—those who really need to see God's power and love? With your partner—or with everyone, after your prayer time—identify one such group. Ask God how he wants you to get involved and how the Spirit could shine through your actions. Consider your passions, your availability, and your location. Work together to identify a practical, meaningful way you can help, and then get to it!

This week I'll take a step toward fulfilling the desires of the Spirit in my life by: _____

_____

_____

_____

After ten minutes, get back together and open up a time of prayer for your group, making sure others have the opportunity to join in.

Ask God to help make the work and the desires of the Spirit more real in each person's life, and that each person will grow deeper in his or her faith and knowledge as they pursue the challenges the Spirit is prompting each of them to tackle.

TURNING ON— AND LIVING IN— THE POWER

7

OVERVIEW

In this session we'll learn how to live and trust in the power of the Holy Spirit—the only real power we have to transform our lives.

The power of sin and death is like the power of gravity. But sin and death can be overcome by an even more powerful force—the Spirit. The Holy Spirit is a rocket that has enough power to propel you beyond the pull of sin. Previously you were a lawbreaker and under condemnation. Now there is a new and greater power, a new law—the law of the Spirit. So since you are free from the power of sin and death, you do not have to give in to sin. You do not have to lie awake at night angry with someone, or wake up angry with them. You do not have to make critical remarks. You do not have to give in to worry and fear. Your life need not be ruled and regulated by sin anymore because you have the all-surpassing power of the Spirit.

Living by the Spirit is the only way to live the Christian life. On the one hand, the Spirit fights against the flesh. On the other hand, the Spirit enables us to fulfill the law. To be sure, there is much freedom in the Christian life, but it is a freedom constrained by the Spirit. It is not a freedom to sin but a freedom to love. If we live by the Spirit we will produce the fruit of the Spirit and not gratify the desires of the flesh. The answer to the question "How do we change?" is quite simple: live by the Spirit!

OPENING THE DISCUSSION

1. Were you ever picked on or harassed by a bully? If so, share a little about that experience. What did you do to keep the bully from bothering you? How successful were you?

2. Whether you have children or not, what advice would you give them about dealing with a bully?

We still have bullies in our lives, don't we? But they're not always people. This week we're going to consider how we can beat a couple other bullies we continue to deal with. The best-known bully of all is Satan, and by extension "against the powers of this dark world and against the spiritual forces of evil in the heavenly realms" (Ephesians 6:12). Our other opponent is our own flesh, in all its selfishness—and as we've already explored throughout this study, that too is a formidable foe.

More important, however, is that even though we're in a battle, Jesus wins. More than that, the Spirit gives us the power we need to live in that victory more and more each day. Let's discover how.

OPENING THE WORD

Get into four subgroups; a "group of one" is okay if necessary. Take fifteen minutes to read your assigned set of verses and discuss the questions that follow.

    a.   Genesis 1:1–3 and 2:7; Job 33:4; and Psalm 33:6 (Note: In the Old Testament, the Hebrew word for *spirit* is also sometimes translated *breath*.)

    b.   Luke 10:21; Acts 10:37–45; and 1 Peter 3:17–18

    c.   John 3:3–8; 2 Thessalonians 2:13–14; and 1 Peter 1:1–2

    d.   Acts 2:1–4, 38–47; 1 Corinthians 12:12–14; and Ephesians 2:19–22

3. What do these verses say about the power and ministry of the Spirit?

4. How do these expressions of the Spirit apply to the challenges *you* regularly face? Give examples.

Come back together after fifteen minutes and share highlights and insights from your discussion time.

We begin to notice, besides our particular sinful acts, our sinfulness; begin to be alarmed not only about what we do, but about what we are. This may sound rather difficult, so I will try to make it clear from my own case. When I come to my evening prayers and try to reckon up the sins of the day, nine times out of ten the most obvious one is some sin against charity; I have sulked or snapped or sneered or snubbed or stormed. And the excuse that immediately springs to my mind is that the provocation was so sudden and unexpected: I was caught off my guard, I had not time to collect myself. Now that may be an extenuating circumstance as regards those particular acts: they would obviously be worse if they had been deliberate and premeditated. On the other hand, surely what a man does when he is taken off his guard is the best evidence for what sort of man he is? Surely what pops out before the man has time to put on a disguise is the truth? If there are rats in a cellar you are most likely to see them if you go in very suddenly. But the suddenness does not create the rats: it only prevents them from hiding. In the same way the suddenness of the provocation does not make me an ill-tempered man: it only shows me what an ill-tempered man I am. The rats are always there in the cellar, but if you go in shouting and noisily they will have taken cover before you switch on the light. Apparently the rats of resentment and vindictiveness are always there in the cellar of my soul.

Now that cellar is out of reach of my conscious will. I can to some extent control my acts: I have no direct control over my temperament. And if (as I said before) what we are matters even more than what we do—if, indeed, what we do matters chiefly as evidence of what we are—then it follows that the change which I most need to undergo is a change that my own direct, voluntary efforts cannot bring about. And this applies to my good actions too. How many of them were done for the right motive? How many for fear of public opinion, or a desire to show off? How many from a sort of obstinacy or sense of superiority which, in different circumstances, might equally had led to some very bad act? But I cannot, by direct moral effort, give myself new motives. After the first few steps in the Christian life we realise that everything which really needs to be done in our souls can be done only by God.

— C. S. Lewis, *Mere Christianity*
New York: Macmillan, 1952; pp. 164–65

Read the passage by C. S. Lewis on page 68, either aloud or quietly on your own. Then read aloud Romans 8:1–39. Afterward, discuss the following questions:

5. What does the law of the Spirit accomplish that the Mosaic law cannot? How are we changed by the Spirit as a result?

6. Where do you most often experience that "hostility" between flesh and Spirit (vv. 6–7)? Or as Lewis might put it, what are the rats in *your* cellar?

7. How do the truths and promises in this passage address those issues? How have you seen the Spirit address those issues already?

"Shall we continue to depend upon our own efforts, or shall we receive by faith the power of God? . . . Struggle as we may, we remain just a part of this evil world until, by faith, we cry: 'Not by might, nor by power, but by Thy Spirit, O Lord of Hosts.'"
— J. Gresham Machen, *What Is Faith?*

OPENING YOUR LIFE

Let's take this a step further—from our battle with the flesh to our battle against the one who facilitated the falling of our flesh in the first place.

Read Ephesians 6:10–18 and answer the following questions:

8. When have you experienced a time of spiritual warfare? What, or who, helped you during that time?

9. Paul refers to several spiritual weapons here. Which do you rely on the most? How? Which of these spiritual weapons could you use an "upgrade" in?

10. Who do you know that really needs someone to fight alongside them spiritually right now—whether they realize they're in a fight or not? How will remembering that it's God's armor, and not ours, affect the way we fight?

Get back into your groups from earlier.

Take ten minutes to review this week's challenges and share which one you'll take on—or if God's used something in this session to inspire you to take on a different "fight." Also make plans to touch base with each other before the next session. Write what you're doing in response to this week's session in the space below.

- Where have you been most susceptible to attack? Sexual tempta- tion? Addiction? The desire for possessions? Commit to avoid- ing situations where temptation is most likely and to praying for that area of your life daily. Also, find someone who'll hold you accountable in that area and help fight spiritually alongside you. You might be sitting with him or her right now!

- Who do you know who seems to be under a great deal of spiritual pressure—even if he or she doesn't know the Spirit? It could be a situation at work, or in your neighborhood. Maybe he or she's facing some kind of harassment, encountering more than the usual amount of temptation, or simply going through a very difficult time. Be sensitive to ways you can support this person, such as sending a note of encouragement or personally inter- vening on his or her behalf—with God and possibly even with other people.

- There are people all around the world in bondage to sin, whether by choice or not. Address one of those needs as a group. Volunteer to help at a crisis-pregnancy center, to help mothers overcome their bondage to guilt and fear. Or raise funds and supplies for a group doing mercy ministry. Check your heart. Then let the Spirit move you forward.

This week I'll let the Spirit take the lead in fighting my battles by:

_____

_____

_____

_____

After ten minutes, get back together and close in prayer.

Ask God to help each person fight the spiritual battles they face and give the wisdom to know how to fight them—for both themselves and others.

BY THEIR FRUIT YOU WILL KNOW THEM

8

OVERVIEW

In this session you'll examine the relationship between the Spirit's work and your obedience, distinguish between good fruit and its counterfeit, and learn why *the Spirit desires to produce good fruit in your life.*

This session will focus on Galatians 5:22–23 with its reference to the fruit of the Spirit. We will explore in greater detail how the Christian life should express itself. We will consider some of the fruit that Paul mentions in Galatians 5:22 (such as joy and gentleness), as well as some not mentioned here, which are also the fruit of the Spirit (such as freedom). More importantly, we'll examine how we can continue to bear good fruit in our lives, and how the Spirit wants to use that fruit to nourish others.

OPENING THE DISCUSSION

10 MINUTES

1. When have you really wanted someone to notice something about you without you having to come right out and say it? What did you do instead to be noticed?

2. On the other hand, when has someone noticed something about you—good *or* bad—that you weren't even thinking about? Share a little about it.

The fruit of our lives is always on display—whether we're looking to show it off or not—so it might as well be good fruit! This session is all about that. We're going to examine the good fruit that the Spirit produces in our lives, what we can do to cultivate it, and why it's worth it.

OPENING THE WORD

Read Galatians 5:13–23. Then discuss:

3. Practically speaking, what does it mean for us to *live by* the Spirit? What does that actually look like? Come up with some ways.

4. Why do you think Paul contrasts "acts" (vv. 19–21) with "fruit" (vv. 22–23)? Is he trying to downplay or ignore our effort in living the Christian life? If so, how?

5. The fruit of the Spirit listed here is a representative list, not an exhaustive one. What other fruit of the Spirit can you think of that's not mentioned in this list?

6. We often view the fruit of the Spirit in terms of "what the Spirit produces in *my* life." What evidences do you see in this passage that the fruit of the Spirit in our lives isn't just for us?

In verse 23, Paul says of the fruit of the Spirit, "Against such things there is no law." This is true. Because Jesus is the fulfillment of the law

(Matthew 5:17), we who have the Spirit's fruit also fulfill the law (Galatians 5:14). There is nothing we need to do apart from or outside of this fruit. Yet we often try to substitute the fruit of our human spirit for the Holy Spirit. And whether it manifests itself as legalism or license, the source is the same: us.

Take turns reading Matthew 23:1–39, then reread Galatians 5:19. Then discuss the following questions:

7. How are legalism and license two sides of the same coin? What examples of that can you see as you compare these two passages?

Give group members a minute to review the "Christian maturity" diagram [Fig. 8.1]. Then go on to question 8.

Figure 8.1

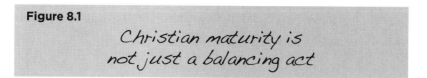

Christian maturity is not just a balancing act

MATURITY

↓

LEGALISM ⟷ LICENSE/ FREEDOM

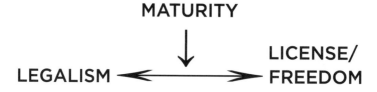

It is believed that Christian maturity is finding the balance between Freedom and Legalism.

Figure 8.2

True Christian maturity

FAITH

LEGALISM/
LICENSE
(Focus on self)

TRUSTING
IN JESUS

LOVE
(Focus
on others)

True Christian maturity is moving
from a focus on SELF to a focus on Jesus,
which then allows us to focus on others.

---

8. How have you seen the truth in these two charts demonstrated in your own life? When has the "balancing act" between legalism and license caused you to fall?

9. Whether it's legalism or license, in what ways do we try to rename—and therefore minimize—our sin and the pain it brings us and others?

10. How does the fruit of the Spirit nullify the need for us to judge or create false laws, *or* break God's law?

*Theologians, philosophers, counselors, and psychologists have all wrestled with the question "How do we change?" Think for a moment about an ingrained sin pattern in your life—whether it's an act of license or legalism—nonetheless, something you're totally powerless against, something you have repeatedly tried to stop doing. Where are you going to get the power to change that? Furthermore, how do we change so that we're not merely altering our outward behavior, but producing fruit that is acceptable to God—since **whatever** is not of faith is sin (Romans 14:23)?*

Paul gives us the answer: If we walk by the Spirit, we will not gratify the desires of the flesh (Galatians 5:16). Every day we live with two realities: the old and the new, the realm of the flesh and the realm of the Spirit. It is a great battle, and the question is, to which reality will we yield? The Spirit is a person with whom we can cooperate, whom we can grieve, on whom we can depend, and to whom we can respond.

OPENING YOUR LIFE

*Let's also remember that the fruit of the Spirit isn't **only** "of the Spirit"—it is also fruit of the Father, and of the Son. And as we do so, let's consider our next steps.*

Read John 15:1–8. Then discuss the following questions:

11. How does abiding in Jesus both produce fruit and eliminate the need to find false ways of producing fruit?

12. Where do you most need to be "pruned" right now, so you can "bear much fruit, showing yourselves to be [Jesus'] disciples"? How will you allow the Spirit to do his work in that area?

Get into groups of three or four.

Take ten minutes to review this week's challenges and share which one you'll take on—or if the Spirit wants to bear fruit in you another way, do that instead. Also, make plans to touch base with each other before the next session. Write what you're doing in response to this week's session in the space below.

- Reflect again on our last question. Take time each day this week to ask yourself "Have I displayed the fruit of the Spirit in my actions and attitudes? Is there any pruning God needs to do in my life? If so, what would it look like?" Consider keeping a journal, to help you reflect on how the Spirit is working through your circumstances and guiding you through them. Share what you've learned during your check-in time with your partners.

- What areas of your life are without the joy of the Spirit? What are some reasons for this lack? How can the gospel speak to this area of your life?

- Where do you sense God calling you to something where you'll be able to clearly say, "There's *no* way I could have done this without the Spirit?" What would be a visible expression of that fruit? Recognizing the fruit is not for the purpose of saying "Look how wonderful I am, thanks to the Spirit," but to take what God's given you and use it for his kingdom. Ask God to show you the next steps and the people he wants to put you with to make those steps happen.

This week I'll bear—and share—the fruit of the Spirit by: _____

_____

_____

_____

Come back together as a group. Take a few minutes to share prayer requests as an entire group, and then pray. As an introduction to your prayer time, read Galatians 5:22–23 again. Then pray that the fruit of the Spirit would become more evident in each person's life, as the Spirit guides and works through each situation you're praying for.

WHERE IS GOD TAKING ME, AND HOW?

9

OVERVIEW

In this session we'll come to a deeper understanding about the goal of our sanctification—an eternal life with Christ—and how the Spirit wants our sanctification to extend beyond us.

Our sanctification—the process by which the Spirit makes us more like Jesus—encompasses a number of goals. In this session we'll consider a few of the major areas. One goal is that we bear fruit; another is that through our sanctification we will testify to the nations. All of it, however, points to one overarching goal: to prepare us—and to use us to prepare others—for eternal life with Jesus. And that eternal life begins *now*.

Our sanctification guides us toward the goal of the new heaven and new earth—which will be crowned with perfect love. We no longer simply want to "be good," but we desire to share the ultimate good of Jesus with the world. Ultimately, all this brings God glory.

As with any journey, while we travel the road of our sanctification, we should always keep our goal and our destination in mind. We'll conclude this session by reviewing where God has taken us, and thinking through where he might be taking each of us next.

OPENING THE DISCUSSION

Since your next session will be your last one in this study, you probably want to start discussing what to do after you're done. Will you move on to one of the other two Gospel Transformation studies, *Gospel Identity* or *Gospel Relationships*? Study another subject? Make plans now, if you haven't already.

1. When have you worked hard to attain a goal? How did it feel as you worked toward it? As you finally attained it? A few months afterward?

2. How did your focus on that goal affect all the other things going on in your life at the time?

*We're in the next-to-last week of this study—we can see the finish line from here. It's a good feeling. But there are far bigger goals God has planned for us. The Spirit is taking us through this lifelong process called sanctification. In this case, the goal isn't just one specific accomplishment. For that matter, our success ultimately won't be based on what **we've** done. So let's explore* *further what sanctification is, what it looks like, and what this process is preparing us for—and let's start at the end.*

OPENING THE WORD

35 MINUTES

Have volunteers read Revelation 21:1–7, 22–27; 22:1–5. Then discuss the following questions:

3. Where are you headed? What will it be like when you get there? What will *you* be like?

You are heading to a place where everything is new: a new life, a new home, and a new world. Nothing will hinder your eternal relationship with Jesus or with others. Your desires will be like Jesus' desires. Finally, you will fully be whom God created you to be. You will delight in loving others. You will love them perfectly, and they you in return. No relationship will ever again be marred, strained, or broken. And you will never again doubt God's great love for you.

*But eternal life is not just reserved for **after** this life. We already have new life in Jesus, and we are called to live it. Through this new life we are being made more like Jesus, even now. On the way to our final destination the Spirit desires to accomplish other goals—to reach the world with the Good News and to bear fruit that will last in our lives and in others' lives. By maintaining an eternal focus, we allow the Spirit to transform everything else in our lives for God's glory. Let's take a closer look at the kind of people God is changing us into—even now.*

Have a volunteer read Philippians 1:4–11, and then discuss the following questions:

4. What does Paul ask God for in his prayer for the Philippians, and for what reasons?

5. When has God used a difficult or challenging situation to produce "a good work in you" (v. 6)? What "knowledge and depth of insight" (v. 9) came out of that experience?

"Disciples do not just believe differently, they behave differently. They stick out. They provoke. They cause people to think. Disciples jar others to evaluate their own lives, often without uttering a word. Disciples point people to the kingdom of God simply by their behavior alone."
— Brian Jones, *Getting Rid of the Gorilla*

Have volunteers read 2 Corinthians 3:9–18; 4:6–18. Then discuss the following questions:

6. Where have you seen God's grace reach "more and more people" (2 Corinthians 4:15)? What role did he allow you to play in that?

7. How does contemplating "the Lord's glory" (2 Corinthians 3:18)—and how *he* chooses to manifest it—help you let go of your own expectations or fears and smile and say, "Okay God, whatever's next—bring it on"?

God has allowed us to experience some incredible things. Even if those experiences may have seemed hard at the time, every experience is an opportunity to give glory to God. God can and will use everything for his good (Romans 8:28)—both the obvious victories and even those things that cause us to suffer and/or seem unexplainable to us—if we'll love and trust him. Let's take a closer look into what that might mean for each of us.

*"To 'grow in grace' means to utilize
more and more grace to live by, until everything
we do is assisted by grace . . . . The greatest saints
are not those who need less grace, but those
who consume the most grace, who indeed are
most in need of grace—those who are saturated
by grace in every dimension of their being.
Grace to them is like breath."*
— Dallas Willard, *Renovation of the Heart*

OPENING YOUR LIFE

*"We do not have to get up into some exalted
state to find Christ, or down into some profound
and terrible experience. We can find Him
everywhere we are . . . . We can take Him
as we are, and He will lead us into all
the experiences we need."*
— A. B. Simpson, *The Fourfold Gospel*

Have everyone get into groups of three or four. Make sure everyone has something to write with.

Let's spend some time reflecting on the times and places God has met us throughout our lives. We've touched on a couple situations already in our discussion time, and even if you didn't share about them, you may have thought of responses. There have probably been other seasons of growth as well. It might have been a "mountaintop" experience, when you knew God was doing incredible things and you were in the middle of it. Or it might have been a time you were in the valley, but God was still especially close. It might even have been a time you didn't know God was working, but looking back you see hints of what God was up to.

On your own, read and work through questions 8–12. Think about when God has been especially present in your life. Write down answers as they come to you. Use your answer to question 12 as your challenge for this week, and write it in the space below.

Take fifteen minutes to work through these questions on your own, and then take another fifteen minutes to share your answers with your group. Set a time to touch base during the week also. Then let's come back together to close in prayer.

8. When have you taken a big step of faith and/or obedience because you knew it was what God wanted? Write down any examples that come to mind.

9. When have you been conscious of God guiding your steps, whether you knew it at the time or realized it later on? Again, write as many responses as you can remember.

10. When have you felt most fulfilled in your walk with Jesus? What was taking place in your life at the time?

11. Now, reflect on your last three answers. Try to review your examples in chronological order, if possible. What patterns, if any, do you see in where God's taken you to this point? How do you see your own desires increasingly reflect God's?

12. Based on what you've written—or even if it's *not* based on what you've written—where do you think God might be trying to take you next? How does *that* reflect God's heart? And what's your next step on that journey?

This week I'll step the next step on the journey that "ends" in eternity by: _____

_____

_____

_____

After thirty minutes, get back together and close in prayer.

> *Lord, we thank you for every experience you've brought into our lives—for things that have fulfilled the desires of our hearts as well as yours, even for things that may have been painful at the time but helped others to see your glory. Lead us where you want us to be next, and reveal your life in us to everyone you put us in contact with. In Jesus' name, amen.*

10 ~~DYING~~ LIVING DAILY IN JESUS

OVERVIEW

In this session you'll recognize that the supreme mark of discipleship—following and imitating Jesus—is dying daily. You'll also look at your daily deaths for evidences of "resurrection."

Christian discipleship may be summed up in one phrase: dying daily. This entire study may be viewed from this perspective. Faith is a form of dying because it means we must choose to believe things that are contrary to what we naturally trust. Repentance means dying, for it requires giving up our cherished desires. Love means dying, for it means giving up our lives for the sake of others.

Fortunately, we do not have to do all this dying on our own. By trusting in the resurrection life we have in Christ, and the work of the Spirit in transforming us, dying daily brings a new kind of life. This session will help us see how following Christ and loving others entails death for us, but life for others.

OPENING THE DISCUSSION

Make sure you have a plan for next week and beyond. Also, have a plan for celebrating your completion of this study and the work God has done in your lives through it. Do something special before or after your gathering time, or plan a separate celebration for another time and place.

So here we are—at the end of this study, but at the beginning of growth that we can't even comprehend yet. Before we get into the heart of today's session, let's take some time to reflect on how God has already grown us over the course of this study.

1. What's been the most meaningful part of this study for you? How have you seen the Spirit already make it more real to you?

2. As the Spirit has been bringing these truths to life, what other things have you found yourself beginning to let go of—*dying to*, we might even say?

As we increasingly walk by the Spirit, we also increasingly cease to gratify the desires of the flesh (Galatians 5:16). We are being changed day by day. And as we die to the works of our flesh and allow the Spirit to lead, we live even more deeply as sons and daughters of God (Romans 8:13–14). Despite what we continue to face in this world, we begin to taste eternal life now and are equipped to share that life with others.

> *"The first Christ-suffering which every man must experience is the call to abandon the attachments of this world . . . . We must face up to the truth that the call of Christ does set up a barrier between man and his natural life."*
> — Dietrich Bonhoeffer, *The Cost of Discipleship*

OPENING THE WORD

Have volunteers read Romans 6:3–11; 2 Corinthians 4:11–12; and Philippians 3:10–14. Then discuss these questions:

3. Does the idea that we're already "always being given over to death" (2 Corinthians 4:11) bother you? If yes, how? Why?

4. On the other hand, what's the freedom "buried" within this truth? Explain.

5. What does it mean to become like Jesus in his death? What evidence of this have you already seen as you've come to know Jesus more deeply?

Let's look at a few examples of what dying daily (our discipleship to Jesus) looks like.

Have volunteers read Luke 9:23–25; John 15:11–17; and Philippians 2:1–11. Then discuss:

6. What does it mean to be a disciple and to imitate Christ? Looking at Jesus' life here and elsewhere, what do you think Jesus expects from us?

7. Practically speaking, how will dying daily work itself out in our lives? What are the daily "resurrections" (a return to life/hope/freedom/joy/love) we can watch for as we live like this?

> "It is easy to die for Christ.
> It is hard to live for him. Dying takes only an hour
> or two, but to live for Christ means to die daily."
> — Sadhu Sundar Singh

We know we're dying daily, and even have some examples of what that looks like. But what will dying daily look like to us and to others, as we live these truths in our relationships? That's what we're going to explore next.

Take a few minutes to work through the following list below on your own. Check any items that you feel particularly relate to your life. We'll discuss as a group afterward.

What might daily death look like?

☐ **Dying in your family.** Moving toward your spouse or child in love when he or she is judging and accusing you will feel like death. Yet intimacy cannot take place without such dying. If you want intimacy with your spouse and children, you will have to die to yourself—to your desires, fears, judgments, and preconceived ideas.

☐ **Dying in your friendships.** Do you have friendships where you sacrifice honesty for comfort? The truth is, a superficial friendship will die out more easily—and a lot more slowly—than a true friendship where you challenge one another (including allowing the other person to challenge *you*) and work through conflicts together.

☐ **Dying in your work.** Perhaps your job is not highly esteemed by the world, and you hear, "Why waste your talents?" Or you want to become a pastor and you hear, "Aren't they just a bunch of crooks and adulterers?" A homemaker may hear, "So when are you going to get a real job?" In each case, you need to die to other people's condemnation. Or, conversely, you may have a highly prestigious job and hear, "That's a very impressive job." In that case, if you start thinking highly of yourself, you need to die to the praise of others.

☐ **Dying to your education, knowledge, and life experience.** Knowledge puffs up. We tend to equate knowledge with godliness. That is why we give out so much information—it looks impressive! What it often is, is a persistent skepticism that dismisses simple truths.

☐ **Dying to people's opinions of you.** To love well, you must die daily to what others think of you. An old woman was asked the question, "What's the best thing about living to be 105?" She replied, "No peer pressure!"

☐ **Dying to your own goals, ambitions, and glory.** We all have our dreams and ambitions, but many times they are contrary to following Jesus. If we are on a quest for our own glory, we are not imitating Christ, for he did not seek his own glory (John 8:54).

☐ **Dying to your own lusts for pleasure, comfort, and control.** When things are going badly, life is boring, or the trials of life affect us, we often fail to love others. Instead, we are thinking about the next thing we can buy, eat, or amuse ourselves with, or trying to find someone else to judge, analyze, or gossip about.

☐ **Dying to your judgment of others.** We must die to our own reputation, rather than defend it by judging others. This will be an ongoing battle. As you grow in your understanding of the gospel, in some ways you will find it harder to love others because you will better understand how other people are failing to love as they ought. Therefore, your capacity to judge others will grow.

☐ **Dying to forms of your own glory.** What are some things that you "credit to your account"? Financial status, lifestyle, personality, gifts, talents, education, beauty, people you know, or heritage? How difficult is it for you to consider these things as a "loss" (Philippians 3:8)?

☐ **Dying to your own reputation.** What matters is who we are before God, so allow God to defend your reputation. Die to shallow apologies, easy confessions, defensiveness, blame-shifting, and excuse-making.

☐ **Dying to (add your own)**_____

_____

_____

_____

_____

Give everyone up to five minutes to work through their list, and then regain everyone's attention. Take five minutes as a group to share some of your answers. Then discuss the following questions:

8. Where is it costing you—or where do you sense it *will* cost you next—to follow Jesus? How will it affect those around you?

*"Nondiscipleship costs abiding peace,
a life penetrated throughout by love,
faith that sees everything in the light of God's
overriding governance for good . . . power to do
what is right and withstand the forces of evil.
In short, it costs exactly that abundance
of life Jesus said he came to bring."*
— Dallas Willard, *Spirit of the Disciplines*

OPENING YOUR LIFE

20 MINUTES

*Let's remember, in all this, that while we are dying daily, we are not **only** dying. In closing this study let's reflect on where Jesus is taking us and what we can look forward to.*

Have volunteers read 1 Corinthians 15:42–57. Then discuss these questions:

9. How does this passage inspire you? Comfort you? Frighten you?

10. How can we reframe our lives so that "the perishable [can] clothe itself with the imperishable, and the mortal with immortality" (v. 53)? How do we allow the Spirit to "sow" into us, so we can more deeply live resurrection life here on earth?

11. How might the Spirit want to use you to sow his life into others as well? Who can help support *you* as you live—and die—daily for Jesus?

"Nothing in you that has not died
will ever be raised from the dead. Look for yourself,
and you will find in the long run only hatred,
loneliness, despair, rage, ruin, and decay.
But look for Christ and you will find Him, and with
Him everything else thrown in."
— C. S. Lewis, *Mere Christianity*

Ask everyone to get into pairs.

Reflect again on our last question. Let's make it our closing challenge for this week—and beyond. Share with your partner how you'll respond to Jesus' command to die daily, and write it in the space below. Also, make plans to touch base with each other before the next session. Let's plan to come back together in five minutes.

This week (and beyond) I'll begin sowing Christ's life into the world by: _____

_____

_____

_____

After five minutes, bring everyone back together. Close in prayer.

Dear God, Thank you for the work you have done and are continuing to do in our lives. Thank you that death has been swallowed up in victory (1 Corinthians 15:54) and that our lives extend far beyond our few years on earth. Help each of us maintain that eternal perspective, as we die daily for Jesus' sake. We pray that we will see the fruit of that dying—that we would witness both our lives and the lives around us transformed by the love of Jesus. Amen.

LEADER'S GUIDE

These answers are suggestions, not definitive responses to the questions. That doesn't mean they're not helpful or accurate, but it does mean your group might come up with better—and very possibly, more personally relevant—answers. So don't rely on this guide to "feed the correct answers" to your group. That will only serve to short-circuit the impact of this course and undermine opportunities for growth in your group members' lives.

*On the other hand, the group might get stuck on one or more questions, especially depending on the maturity level of your members. In which case we're here to help. But again, don't use these answers as a crutch or a shortcut; wrestle with the questions together as a group **first** before looking at these answers.*

If you choose to use these answers as part of your regular discussion, we suggest the following format:

1. **Discover.** First, come up with your own complete answers to the questions using the Scripture passages, session content, diagrams, and your own personal and collective encounters with Jesus as a springboard. You need to discover the answers for yourself to get the most out of this study. As group leader, be sure to facilitate this type of learning and discussion.
2. **Direct.** *Now* review, study, and discuss the suggested answers and reflections at the back of the manual.
3. **Rediscover.** Once you've reflected on both your answers and ours, spend time as a group talking about further ideas or questions that arise. Return to your original answers and write down any new insights, thoughts, and applications.

Good luck! May God grow you together!

SESSION 1: WHAT MAKES A CHRISTIAN GROW?

1. Answers will vary, and they don't all have to be "spiritual." The growth of our kids or the flowers in our garden can also be great illustrations of the kind of growth the Spirit wants to perform within us. Growth can be amazing; growth can also hurt a lot. Growth almost always takes time. Don't dismiss *anyone's* answers here.

2. Answers will vary. Very likely people's growth spurts will involve a change in involvement, in perspective, in the reality of God's presence in their lives, or all of the above. Encourage people to share what God has already done in their lives.

3. We can describe faith as our spiritual eyesight. Faith is opening our eyes to what God has done, is doing, and will do. It is living in light of these truths. It is seeing what God is like. It is seeing who we are in light of the gospel. Faith entails accepting that what God says about us is true. It is trusting that he is wise, good, loving, and in control. Jesus told his disciples in John 6:29, " 'The work of God is this: to believe in the one he has sent.' " By believing, we receive the Spirit and his fruit by faith. Nonetheless, we can short-circuit the work of the Spirit by our own unbelieving effort. "Are you so foolish? After beginning with the Spirit, are you now trying to attain your goal by human effort?" (Galatians 3:3).

4. Answers will vary.

5. We struggle with self-deception and self-righteousness. Our hearts naturally slide in this direction. We instinctively gravitate toward un-believing effort because we think we have power in and of ourselves to produce change. Sometimes, when we speak about the fruit of the Spirit we isolate it from a vibrant faith. The dynamic "Faith → Spirit → Fruit" is important. The fruit comes from the Spirit, and the Spirit is received by faith. Missing this dynamic can easily turn a discussion of the fruit of the Spirit into an exhortation to produce these fruit apart from faith, dependence, and repentance.

6. Faith must come first. We cannot earn God's grace by our good works. However, because of God's grace we are empowered to do the good works *he* has created and called us to do (Ephesians 2:10). And if we

are obedient to God, that work will get done. Our good works, then, are nothing we can boast in, but something only fully accomplished by the work of the Spirit.

7. The Spirit supplies the power for us to live the Christian life. Faith is a mere instrument in God's working in and through us. Faith, like prayer, is not powerful in of itself. If faith is powerful, it is only because it is God's instrument for receiving the Spirit (Ephesians 1:19–20).

8. The same power that raised Christ from the dead and seated him in the heavenly realms is available to believers now. By faith, this power is for those who believe (v. 19). It is important to stress that faith is not the power. Rather, faith is more like a "switch" that allows the Spirit's power to flow into our lives. Only the Spirit has the power to throw mountains into the sea, raise the dead, and create the world. One amazing truth of the gospel is that this great power is at work in our lives—those who believe!

9–10. Answers will vary.

SESSION 2: WHO DO YOU SAY I AM— AND DO YOU BELIEVE IT?

1. Answers will vary.

2. Answers will vary. More than likely they'll include answers like strength, speed, vitality, and intelligence. In many cases the implication is that if we align ourselves with this team or use this product, we too will be strong, fast, full of life, smarter—in short, something better than what we are.

3. Our symbol, as Christians, is the cross of Jesus Christ. God took something that once struck dread into the hearts of people and transformed it into a symbol of life, reconciliation, and hope. As a foundational symbol, the cross teaches us that the kingdom takes the things of this world and turns them upside down—the last will be first and the first last; the humble will be exalted, the proud cast down. Philosophies and ideologies have risen and fallen. Kingdoms of this world come and go. However, the message of the cross remains. That the Lord's Supper is celebrated throughout the world today is a testimony to this abiding message. The kingdom of God is growing, while the Roman Empire is long gone.

The Messiah did not come as a triumphant king but as a suffering servant. Suffering was something that he experienced not once, but many times. Jesus was a man familiar with suffering (Isaiah 53:3). Isaiah speaks about a new age for the people of God (Isaiah 42:1–9; 49:1–13; 50:4–9; 52:13—53:12). It is an age where suffering servanthood, not rulership, is a sign of election. Now we must pass through many trials and pain before we will enter the kingdom of God (Acts 14:22). The cross is a message that says that the path to glory is through suffering. The entire Christian life is now summed up with Jesus' words, "If anyone would come after me, he must deny himself and take up his cross daily and follow me" (Luke 9:23). Jesus' death becomes the pattern for our lives.

4. Jesus ransomed us from slavery to the world and our sin. Jesus restored our fellowship with God by his work on the cross. Because of Jesus, we can now enjoy a right relationship with God. We have received forgiveness through Christ, who has disarmed the principalities and powers of darkness. By his death and resurrection, Jesus takes away the main weapon of principalities and powers—death. Rome ruled through the fear of death, and the cross was a symbol of that as well. And behind earthly powers is Satan who keeps people in bondage through their fear of death (Hebrews 2:14–15). But Jesus saves us from all of it. Through the cross, we see the love of God (Romans 5:8) and the love of Jesus (Galatians 2:20).

5. Because I have been crucified with Christ, the benefits of his death are mine. Christ now lives in me. His Spirit dwells within me. I now live this life by faith. I do not set aside the grace of God because righteousness cannot be gained apart from faith. We no longer have to live in fear and bondage. But because we are now slaves of Christ (1 Corinthians 7:22) we are called to serve others, to both tell them and reveal to them through our own lives the freedom available in Christ.

6. Answers will vary.

7. Answers will vary. The important thing is for group members to acknowledge this gap exists, and that only Christ can address it. The exercise in Opening Your Life will draw this point out further.

8–10. Answers will vary.

SESSION 3: WASTING TIME WITH GOD

1–2. Answers will vary.

3. Answers will vary. Or answers may not come at all, just a stunned silence. If so, that's okay—let the silence hang out there before moving on. It may be that group members have never thought of time with God as something to be "enjoyed." And yet, the opening words of the Westminster Catechism ring loud and true: "Q: What is the chief and highest end of man? A: Man's chief and highest end is to glorify God, *and fully to enjoy him forever.*"

4. By remaining in Jesus, we are able to bear fruit in our lives. In fact, we can do nothing without him (John 15:5). Without remaining in Jesus, we wither. We're burned up—and more than likely, burned out. But if we remain in him, we can ask anything and it will be done (John 15:7) because we are operating out of his will. Being in Jesus' presence is more important than anything we can do for him (Luke 10:42), and in fact prepares us for the work he really *does* want us to do. Jesus spent time praying to the Father before embarking on outward ministry and before choosing the twelve (Mark 1:35–39; Luke 6:12–13).

5. Over the course of time, the Holy Spirit awakens us—or needs to reassure us—of the objective realities of our faith: God loves us, Jesus has died and paid the price for us, and so on. The ways we spend time during that season of life often reflect that. God will call us to times of quiet when our identities get too wrapped up in "doing." We'll spend more time in our Bibles when we're acutely aware of our need for wisdom. And so on. The Father knows what we need before we ask, and the Spirit will guide us into ways to receive it.

6. Answers will vary.

7. In Jesus' day there were examples of people who distorted the spiritual disciplines of Scripture reading, prayer, fasting, and tithing. Jesus rebuked people for 1) reading the Scriptures yet missing out on him (John 5:39–40); 2) empty and repetitious prayer (Matthew 6:7); 3) fasting to put on a show (Matthew 6:16–18); and 4) tithing while neglecting justice (Luke 11:42). This provides a warning to us that we can slip into relationally disconnected spiritual activities.

8. There are three primary ways this truth manifests itself. See if anything sounds familiar here:

a. **A lack of attention to intimacy.** I know that spending time with him is good for me. I know that I should do it. I know that I would be better if I did. But I just don't do it for a variety of reasons (lazy, busy, tired, something else matters more, and so on).

b. **Basic unbelief.** My circumstances have started to determine my relationship with God. Things are hard, or I'm disappointed, or God doesn't seem to listen to me, or things in my life are changing and so I feel distant. Essentially God is not relating to me on *my* terms, and so I don't believe that he really loves me, that he can or will change things in my life, or that he (and he alone!) can truly satisfy me.

c. **A deep-seated desire to please God through our own righteousness.** When it comes to issues of intimacy with God, this plays out by taking things like Bible reading, prayer, and personal worship and making them do something that they were never intended to do—demonstrate my "merit" to God. If I miss a day or two of prayer or sitting in Scripture, instead of feeling like I really miss my Dad, I feel guilty. Sometimes spending time with God even makes me feel resentful because I feel like I have so much to get done and I "have to" take time away from these other events to be with him or he'll be disappointed with me. What ends up happening is that we take these "intimacy building practices" and use them as measuring sticks of God's approval.

9. Answers will vary.

10. We need time with God. We can't grow without it. For most of us this means we need to be intentional about making it happen. But as with all good relationships, variety is essential. As long as you're truly listening, truly speaking, truly worshiping, there is no one right way to do this. And because the goal of these activities is ongoing intimacy, we should expect to do them in different forms and regularly pursue new things to keep the channels of intimacy open.

SESSION 4: BUT ARE YOU *REALLY* SORRY?

1. Answers will vary.

2–4. For each passage, answers follow:

- Micah 6:1–8—God required from the Israelites a repentant lifestyle, humility, love toward others. They, on the other hand, thought they needed to do something tangible, material, and outward. The level of sacrifices verbally offered progresses from the simple to the absurd—burnt offerings and year-old calves to thousands of rams, ten thousand rivers of oil, even their first-born. God wants none of it. The Israelites have been deceived into thinking that they *have* something to offer. They have forgotten that God gave them everything. Who gave them all the things they want to offer anyway?

- 1 Samuel 15:1–3, 7–31—Saul completes most of the command. He destroys most of the people, but spares Agag and the best animals. He convinces himself he has obeyed the Lord. The heart of the issue is Saul's stubbornness. Saul is arrogant and idolatrous, yet Saul's words contain no mention of these sins. When Saul first sees Samuel, Saul is filled with boastful words; he cannot understand why Samuel is on his case. "I may have missed a few details, but overall, I did a good job." When Saul finally owns up to his sin, he recognizes the underlying idolatry in his life—his fear of the people. Saul even asks for forgiveness. On the surface, his response may be remorseful and regretful, but it is not repentant. However, the issue is not so much that Saul has been caught violating a command, but that his life is in rebellion against God. Saul is still only concerned about saving face before the people. He is not broken over his sin and arrogance, but over his failure in the eyes of others.

- Matthew 26:23–25, 47–50; 27:3–5—Even the outward appearance of Judas' response is lacking many essential elements of true repentance. He is still very much self-centered rather than Christ-centered. He hates Jesus. He is greedy—a lover of money rather than others. He uses Jesus for his own advantage and gain, thus he is adulterous. Yet as with Saul, we do not hear Judas acknowledge any of this in his "repentance." His sinful plan, which all along has been focused on himself, has turned out badly. "He was seized with remorse" (v. 3). Judas returned the money (v. 3). He showed that he no longer wanted to be a part of this whole scheme. He said, "I have sinned…I have betrayed innocent blood" (v. 4). But even when he makes restitution, he is saying, "Take this money so I can feel innocent again. Take the money. Justify me, and get me off the hook." When this fails, he throws the money into the temple and hangs himself. Judas is still controlling his life, and is still unrepentant. Judas was sorry, but there are two kinds of sorrow. The issue is not whether we are sorry, but what kind of sorrow we have (see 2 Corinthians 7:9–10).

5. The main point is that we will *do* anything rather than repent. The people in these passages are ruled by the flesh. The flesh would rather offer its firstborn than walk humbly with God. The flesh says, "What does God want after all? Tell me Lord, and I will give it. If it is ten thousand rivers of oil, I will do it. But don't ask me to repent." The flesh assumes that God demands too much, and yet wants to buy God off as cheaply as possible. Behind all the actions of these people is a desire to change God and get him to accept them on their own terms. They refuse to change; God must change—God is the one who must repent!

False repentance emphasizes the consequences of sin, such as "hurting you." Here I have owned up to what my sin has done to you—hurt you. Yet I have said nothing about the hateful, condemning, sarcastic, and critical words *I* used. This way, I can quickly move to *your* responsibility to forgive me, all the while making it sound like I am repentant!

6. Answers will vary.

7. David owns up to his sin. He uses a variety of Old Testament terms for sin—iniquity, transgression, evil. He sees what is sometimes called "the sinfulness of sin." Not only has he *done* sinful things, he also speaks of his fallen nature. There is a deep conviction of sin without any excuses. The eyes of his heart have been opened. He sees what he did not see before. David is broken. He is now in the place of weakness and powerlessness, hence his plea for help. He does not come to the Lord presuming, demanding, or insisting upon his rights or powers as king (as Saul did

earlier). There is a deep change in David, as is evident in the change in tone from demanding to pleading.

8. David has a strong desire to be in renewed fellowship with God. His turning is dramatic and without pretense (see Jeremiah 3:10). David now acknowledges that God desires truth in his heart (Psalm 51:10, 17). From there, truly good works can spring up, out of a heart that's obedient to God.

9. Kenneth Bailey, in *The Cross and the Prodigal*, argues that at this point the younger son has not really repented at all, but merely come up with "plan b" to get out a tight spot and set himself on the road to recovery. The return, the proposed speech, and the plan to become a hired man all seem calculated to help him move ahead. In any case, no mention of sorrow, repentance, or acknowledgement of the emotional wounds that the younger son has caused are mentioned.

Timothy Keller, in *The Prodigal God*, counters: "The younger son had disgraced his family and…intends to say: 'Father, I know I don't have a right to come back into the family. But if you apprentice me to one of your hired men so I can learn a trade and earn a wage, then at least I could begin to pay off my debt'.…There in the pigsty the younger son rehearses his speech. When he feels he is ready for the confrontation, he…begins the journey home" ([New York: Dutton, 2008], 21).

However imperfect it may have been, the prodigal son repented after a grievous situation that came about because of his sins, and his father welcomed him back with open arms. Often, it is precisely when we are exposed and shamed that we wake up and come to our senses. God often uses difficult circumstances, suffering, and courageous people to precipitate our repentance. God awaits our return so that he can lavish his love upon us.

10. Of course, our repentance does not have to be perfect. Our repentance as well as our faith needs sanctification. A true turning towards God (vertical) is evidenced by our turning towards the people we have wronged (horizontal), whether by paying back what we have stolen (like Zacchaeus in Luke 19:8), or by repenting for our arrogance and coldness, and not just for "fighting with you" or "hurting you."

11. Answers will vary.

12. Often pain is the real currency of repentance. Until we see how much our sin has hurt someone else, we are unlikely to repent in deepening ways. This is why it is so important to listen to those we have sinned against. Often, in hearing how they experienced our sin, we will also gain more insight into the deeper issues of unbelief that were going on in our hearts at the time.

SESSION 5: STARTING OVER— GOD'S WAY

1–2. Answers will vary.

3. In a word, pride. By avoiding repentance, we remain in control. We avoid the pain genuine repentance requires because we don't truly think genuine repentance *is* required to fix what's wrong in our lives. By living in a state of false or non-repentance we keep ourselves on the throne of our lives rather than live faithfully and trustingly toward God.

4. Repentance is different from its fruit (Matthew 3:8). Repentance is foundational to the Christian life. Along with faith, repentance is the instrument God uses to make us more like Christ. In fact, it occupies a similar place to that of faith. In other words repentance, the flip side of faith, works to produce all the things that faith produces. God dwells with the contrite. He gives grace to the humble (Proverbs 3:34). He saves the humble (2 Samuel 22:28). He lifts up the humble. He opposes the proud parent, friend, husband, or wife (James 4:6). To the repentant and humble, God pours out his love, forgiveness, mercy, and salvation. Repentance is central to the transformation of our lives, for it is central to a continuing relationship with God. It is not peripheral or optional.

5. When we humbly sacrifice everything we are to God, God changes everything. Conversely, a person who lives a life of pretense (false humility) loses connection with Jesus, and as a result cannot grow. The negative example provided in Colossians reinforces what we have seen so far: repentance and spiritual growth are organically related. One goal of a life of false humility is to get *other* people to repent! For example, we may think when someone repents to us, "You are wrong; therefore I must be right and, boy, does that feel good!" In this case we are living by others' repentance because it makes us look and feel good.

6. Being a living sacrifice means that with our lives we declare ourselves dead to our sin (Romans 6:11). We no longer insist on our own way. Through humility, we put ourselves in the same boat with the people we used to separate ourselves from, because we no longer think of ourselves as better than them. And because of that, we no longer desire to see that boat sink. We now want to lift others up as well, instead of tearing them down.

7. If faith is receiving, repentance is giving up. I must do more than simply receive the truths that Jesus is the only Savior and the Spirit is the only power; I must also give up my belief that I am my own savior. Either my reputation (my view, or other people's view of my record) or the record of Christ (his reputation) is my life and confidence. I cannot build and protect my own record and live by faith at the same time. I cannot serve two masters (Matthew 6:24). To receive one, I have to give up the other. I will not be changed if I merely believe, without repenting.

8. Once I give up my broken self, I am open to receive—and exhibit—Christ's beauty. To dine at Christ's banquet, I must first die to self. That is the price of admission. If faith means receiving the truths of the gospel into our hearts, then I cannot receive these truths apart from giving up falsehood. For example, when I am acting like God in my home, desiring to control and order everything and everyone in it, it is impossible to receive the truth that God is in control and God orders the world for my good. To receive it, I must give up believing that I am in control.

9. A repentant/humble person is at rest. Satan cannot successfully accuse us (Revelation 12:10). After all, what's the worst that can happen? There is no reputation to protect or achieve, no scheming, no gossip, and no one to manipulate. Nevertheless, it is not where we like to be. By nature, we all think that the last thing we really need is the gospel. At the very least, we think someone else needs it more than we do. Ever listened to a sermon and thought, *If only "so-and-so" were listening—they really need to hear this?* This is not the place of rest, for our minds are filled with schemes for other people.

God dwells with the humble, for God *is* humble. The father of the prodigal runs and humiliates himself (Luke 15:20). Jesus humbles himself to death on a cross (Philippians 2:8). We are to learn from Christ, for he is gentle and humble in heart (Matthew 11:29). He did not come to seek his own glory; he did nothing from himself; his words were not from himself; he did not come to do his own will. He surrendered everything to his Father. Humility is the life and character of God. To be proud is to be anti-God. It is not only to be against God, but also to be unlike God.

Every day, therefore, is to be a mini-conversion. Believe and repent! Tongue in cheek, we might ask, "Who are the largest unreached people group in the world?" Christians! We may have heard the gospel ten years ago, but we need to hear it again. The gospel needs to reach our hearts every day. Like manna in the desert, this bread from heaven must be collected again and again each new day.

SESSION 6: WHO IS THE SPIRIT, AND WHAT DOES HE WANT?

1. Answers will vary.

2. The Spirit is the one who brings new life. The Holy Spirit renews our minds (Romans 12:2), transforms our lives, enables us to see the truth, sets us free from the power of sin (Romans 8:2), gives us understanding, and removes the veil from our hearts. He is the one who sanctifies us, produces fruit in our lives, and fights against the flesh. The Spirit helps us in our weaknesses, helps us to pray, and intercedes for us (Romans 8:26). We receive the Spirit of sonship by which we cry out to God, "Father!" The Spirit testifies to our spirit that we are God's children (Romans 8:15–16).

3. The Spirit enables us to live in dependence on God as we eagerly await our final adoption and redemption. He gives us perseverance (Romans 8:1–5). The Spirit works in us to produce obedience from the heart (Ezekiel 36:26–27), openness, conviction, freedom to own up to our sin, freedom to love. Where the Spirit is, there is freedom (2 Corinthians 3:17).

4. Answers will vary.

5. Answers will vary. Take your time with this question. Acknowledge the struggles people may have with understanding who the Spirit is and his distinct but equal role in the Trinity. Share an example of when the Spirit "turned the light on" for you concerning his role in your life—or how you still have difficulties fully grasping aspects of the Spirit. There

will be additional opportunities to share about the Spirit's real presence in your life when you discuss question 8.

6–7. Individual examples will vary. We begin the Christian life by the Spirit, as we repent and believe the good news. Yet many quickly forget that we are to continue living by the Spirit, as we continue to believe and repent. Unless we continually receive the truths of the gospel, and give up our unbelief, we start to die spiritually. We often try to "store up" Christ from yesterday or ten years ago. We want yesterday's faith and repentance to bring us Christ and his grace today. Like the Israelites in the desert, we find that our manna goes rotten if we try to keep it in our tents. We forget that all the Israelites in the desert died because of their lack of ongoing faith and repentance (Hebrews 4:2).

The focus of Galatians is not being saved or gaining a right standing before God. Rather, it is maintaining and sustaining a right standing before God and others. Is that accomplished by faith or by law?

Think of a vacuum cleaner with a burned-out motor. The vacuum was designed to do something, but it can't. It's broken—useless. When God forgives us through Christ's work on the cross, he removes the broken motor. When he justifies us through Christ he gives us a brand new motor **and** plugs us into the power source that will make our new motor work—the motor of Christ's righteousness and the "electricity" of the Holy Spirit. We need both—Christ's righteousness and the Holy Spirit's enabling power—to live out God's purpose of glorifying God and enjoying him in ways that bring Christ to others. When we try to rely on our own power (i.e. our own willpower or human effort), we're like an unplugged vacuum. We can do nothing when we are not connected to our power source.

8. Individual examples will vary. What does it mean to live by the Spirit? At the very least, Paul says, it means living by faith. We find the power of the Spirit not through the law, not through unbelieving effort, but by humbly believing the gospel. We are changed by yielding ourselves to the Spirit, which is nothing less than yielding to the truth of the gospel—that we are sinners in desperate need of help, but that in Christ we are a new creation in whom Jesus delights.

9. Even in the midst of a difficult situation, the Spirit is with Jesus, helping,

guiding, and empowering him. Even though the Spirit may take us into difficult situations, he is always with us. Whether he takes us into a new situation or keeps us from a new situation, he is always with us. Even in the valley of the shadow of death, he is with us (Psalm 23:4). Because of the Spirit's power and presence, there is no situation that can rob us of faith and obedience.

10. Seeking the wisdom of other Christians, especially those who have spent time walking before God with integrity, is never a bad idea (Proverbs 11:3). At the same time, other Christians are still human. The Spirit may be leading you into a new work that others may not understand at first. Yet the Spirit of truth will guide you into all truth (John 16:13). We need to listen to wise counsel and be open to the fresh movement of the Spirit in our lives.

11. Life in the Spirit is a life firmly connected to an ongoing humble reliance on Jesus. We want to do the right thing, but very often *we* don't know what the right thing *is*. Oddly enough, this is often when our prayer becomes most effective—when we're empty, when we have no agenda except, "Not my will, but yours." This doesn't mean we sit around passively, waiting for God to move us. We can be actively willing. We can do the things we planned, but hold onto them loosely, with the attitude that should the Spirit lead elsewhere, *that's* where we should go (Acts 16:6–8).

A couple practical ideas of what this might look like follow: Search the Bible for wisdom regarding your particular issue, and compare it with what you're feeling led to do. Approach prayer with an attitude of listening for the Spirit, as opposed to simply presenting your list of demands and leaving, or looking for God to rubber-stamp your own desires by saying, "Well, I've prayed over it," without waiting to really hear God answer.

SESSION 7: TURNING ON—AND LIVING IN—THE POWER

1–2. Answers will vary.

3. Among the answers you can expect from your groups:

   a. We see the power of the Spirit in creation. We usually acknowledge that the Father and Son were involved in creation. Often, however, the work of the Spirit is minimized or ignored. The work of creation is Trinitarian. Here in these verses we see that the great power of the Spirit is involved in creating the universe, the earth, and all forms of life, including ourselves. The Spirit's great power is seen in the beauty and majesty of creation. Every part of creation displays the power of the Spirit.

b. We see the power of the Spirit in Jesus' ministry. Jesus overcame temptation by the Spirit! Note the references to the Spirit that encapsulate the passage. Jesus was full of the Spirit, was led by the Spirit, and lived in the joy of the Spirit. Certainly, Jesus relied on the indwelling power of the Spirit.

c. We see the power of the Spirit in redemption. It is the Spirit who convicts of sin, creates new life, and regenerates. He brings joy, hope, and peace. It is the work of the Spirit to produce in us repentance and faith—even these are gifts from God. No one can say "Jesus is Lord," except by the Spirit (1 Corinthians 12:3).

d. We see the power of the Spirit in the Church. The Spirit first created the church at Pentecost, and now he empowers it, equips it with gifts, guides it, and governs it. The Spirit breaks down the entrenched barriers between young and old, slave and free, Jew and Gentile, man and woman. The Spirit unifies the church, and sustains that union through love. God pours his love into our hearts by the Spirit.

4. In a fallen world given to death and decay, it is the Spirit who recreates and renews. We need the strength of the Spirit to surmount every satanic temptation, just as Jesus' human nature did. Because of the wonderful work of the Spirit, we who share the gospel message do not need to speak with wise and persuasive words, but simply be faithful and allow the Spirit to do his convicting work (1 Corinthians 2:4; 1 Thessalonians 1:5). The Spirit even creates fellowship among a bunch of sinners—namely, his church. *That* is considerable power!

5. The Mosaic law was powerless to change the people of God. However, those who walk according to the Spirit will fulfill the requirement of the law. The gospel is very good news. Where the flesh and the law failed, God succeeds by sending his Son and giving his Spirit to his people. Even

Jesus needed the Spirit to live and accomplish his mission. If Jesus had not given you his Spirit, and did not continue to give you his Spirit, you would have no power over sin in your life. You would have no power to obey. To produce the fruit of the Spirit you need the Spirit!

The Spirit is the operative power that enables us to live out the gospel and frees us from sin. Paul's critique of the Mosaic law is that it could not bring about righteousness. In fact, as Paul says elsewhere, the law actually made the situation worse (Romans 7:8–11). What we need is supernatural change and empowerment. From one perspective, all of Romans 8 deals with how the Holy Spirit applies Jesus Christ and his work in the life of the believer.

6. Answers will vary.

7. Personal examples will vary. We change by the Spirit's work of empowering, equipping, transforming, fighting against our flesh. This change, however, is not automatic. We have to live in a posture of repentant faith, the place of humility, the place God delights to bless. We have to make every effort to love. Living by the Spirit does *not* mean a life of no effort or struggle. However, it must be an effort coming from a humble and ongoing trust in Jesus. Since we know that we are intimately loved by God and free from condemnation, we can be sure that he has also provided all the resources we need to live the Christian life. He knows our weaknesses and what we need.

8. Answers will vary.

9. Answers will vary. Paul uses the metaphor of God's armor, which consists of a number of pieces. Yes, there are evil powers, but central to the story is God's armor: his faithfulness, righteousness, truthfulness, and salvation. God has been faithful to his people, and he will continue to be truthful. God is righteous and is putting the whole world right.

10. Personal examples will vary. Nonetheless, we must remember that it is not *our* armor. Sometimes people subtly switch this around, so that the story becomes centered on us—our faith, our righteousness, and so on, until, like David in Saul's armor, we are immobilized and unable to fight! This is not Paul's emphasis. God himself comes to protect you. God himself comes to fight.

So in order for you to fight the battle, you have to take up the Word of God and believe it to be true. This is different from saying, "Oh, here are my weapons! Let me pick them up—my faith, my righteousness, my Bible—and then ride off like a lone knight into battle." Rather, it is a call to center yourself around who God is and what he is doing. It is believing these different aspects of the gospel story: that God is righteous, faithful, and true. That is how you battle these evil forces standing against you—how you are to be strong *in the Lord*, and in his power. You and I are now a part of God's story. Your individual story fits into a grander plan that extends before and beyond your seventy-odd years on this planet.

SESSION 8: BY THEIR FRUIT YOU WILL KNOW THEM

1. Answers will vary. We all have ways of trying to position ourselves to be "caught doing something right." But in so doing, we are all too much like the Pharisees who made their spiritual works of giving and praying so comically obvious. We may not have someone blow a trumpet to announce our goodness, but nonetheless we go out of our way to claim our reward in full rather than allow God to notice and reward us (Matthew 6:2–3).

2. Answers will vary.

3. Part of the fruit of the Spirit in Jesus' life was joy. He delighted in what his Father was doing. He delighted to see that God works through the outcast, the weak, and ignorant. Likewise, you are forgiven, loved, and delighted in. Now you can cry, "Abba, Father!" God is working all things to make you like Jesus. He is using people like yourself. So even in difficult times, you can have the quiet confidence, deep joy, and a settled peace that God is for you, with you, and won't let you down.

As one more example of the fruit of the spirit, gentleness means showing consideration for the people in your life, enabling you to reach out to other sinners. Gentleness is the opposite of pride, arrogance, harshness, and self-assertion. It involves a willingness to bear the burdens of others. The Spirit of Christ produces the fruit of gentleness because that is what Jesus is like. Therefore, you are also called to restore others gently (Galatians 6:1). Those entangled in sin are no different from you. This process will take time. It will take place according to God's schedule and not your own.

4. Paul's use of words is intentional. The "acts," or "works," are done by the flesh. These include works of legalism or licentiousness. They may be obviously evil or counterfeit fruit. You give a lot of thought to "works"— what you have done, what you have worked for. "Fruit" implies a different idea. Fruit is something that is produced in you. This fruit is a natural by-product, a harvest, of a life controlled and guided by the Spirit. The origin of this fruit is supernatural; it is spiritual fruit. Moreover, when you think of fruit, you think of *life*! This is part of the abundant life that Jesus promised his disciples (John 10:10).

5. Among the possible answers: freedom (2 Corinthians 3:17), goodness, righteousness and truth (Ephesians 5:9), forgiveness, growth in the knowledge of God (Colossians 1:10), hope, compassion, an ongoing spirit of repentance (Luke 3:8), unity, humility, a true (not false) spirit of prophecy, and leadership (Matthew 7:15–20).

6. Although the works of the flesh are obvious, the fruit of the Spirit can also be visibly seen or surmised here: the Galatians are called to "serve one another in love" (Galatians 5:13), love their neighbors themselves, and thus fulfill the law (v. 14). We will not become conceited, provoking and envying each other (v. 26), but rather find ways to build one another up.

7. Although outwardly they may have differing characteristics, at heart, legalism and license are the same thing. Both involve looking after "self," and both are idolatrous. There are elements of self-justification, self-glorification, self-deception, and self-gratification in both. The Pharisees piled *their* law on others, while neglecting God's law— "they do not practice what they preach" (Matthew 23:3). They flattered themselves and wanted others to do the same (vv. 5–7); they denied others entrance into heaven (v. 13); they gave exactingly instead of joyfully and to those who needed it (v. 23). On the outside they looked good, but were filled with greed and self-indulgence (v. 25). In short, the Pharisees are "Galatians 5:19 men" waiting to happen, as they are every bit as fleshly and self-centered as those who commit "obvious" acts of the flesh.

8. Answers will vary. Both legalism and license bring curses into our lives, and we despair when they don't bring the life and satisfaction they've promised. While we might think we're simply overcompensating in one

direction or another, the fact is, we are relying on our flesh instead of the Spirit in both cases.

9. Answers will vary, but here are a few examples to get you started: "I'm not angry, I'm disappointed." "It's not lust; I'm just admiring." "I wish I could help you, but I need this money (to *feel* secure, since I rely more on my possessions than on God)." "I'm busy (which often means, I'm too important to make time for you)."

10. Because the law has been fulfilled, the Spirit gives us freedom. Here are just a small sampling of the ways that freedom manifests itself: freedom from the guilt, bondage, power, and corruption of sin; freedom of conscience; freedom from legalistic tyranny; freedom from unlimited obligation; freedom from trying to obey God in our own strength; freedom from doing things to try to win God's favor or others' approval; freedom from having to change people; freedom from pleasing the flesh; freedom to own up to our sins and repent; freedom to walk in the Spirit; freedom to keep the commands of God; freedom to love others. With all that freedom, who *wants* laws?

11. This is a great question, especially if we raise the stakes by trying to apply it to an area where change seems impossible. How do we love God and neighbor with all our hearts, when we love ourselves with all our hearts? Abiding *in* Jesus puts the focus *on* Jesus, instead of where we stand in comparison to others. Trying to "be good" on our own is like stapling our own fruit onto the vine—it may look similar from a distance, but it's not the same up close and it starts rotting right away. And our false, rotten fruit becomes more obvious as time passes. If you are concerned about what people think of you, you are in bondage to them. You may withdraw rather than enter into their world, for fear they will think badly of you. Or you may attack others because you believe it is up to you to change them. In either case you have slipped into slavery and a lack of love.

But you have been set free, not to indulge yourself, but to love others (Galatians 5:13). Once you know that you are truly free, you can begin to love others. By abiding in Christ we draw the strength to bear fruit, and to help others bear fruit.

12. Answers will vary.

SESSION 9: WHERE IS GOD TAKING ME, AND HOW?

1–2. Answers will vary, but they'll likely follow a pattern like this: the time of "working toward the goal" will be at turns difficult and richly rewarding; the immediate elation upon attaining the goal will likely be followed by feelings of dissatisfaction or letdown—"Is this all there is?" "What's the next thing?" and so on. And chances are, the more the goal focuses on us, the more up-and-down our feelings will go. Again, there's no "right" answer to these questions; welcome them all.

3. We are heading to the land of our true citizenship—heaven. We may desire to go to heaven because there is no more pain (which is great), because we will be reunited with many of our loved ones there (which is also great). However, if Jesus were not in heaven, heaven would not be heaven! Without Jesus, we would have nothing—nothing at all. The beauty of this city is Christ. Everything else that is beautiful is a reflection of his beauty, glory, and love. When Jesus comes and touches the earth, it will become new. Everything will blossom. The trees will sing because the Lord has come to reign. Creation will reach its fullest potential.

The difference between what we are now and what we will become is like the relationship between a seed and a flower. The new life is in the seed. The seed dies and is resurrected as a flower. Now you are like the seed; then you will sprout and flower. Now you have the first fruits; then you will have the full harvest. Now you have a taste of freedom; then you will have been brought into the glorious freedom of the children of God (Romans 8:21). Perhaps we will say to each other, "I think I remember you. I remember you from those moments when your beauty shone through! Yes, that was you. You were hidden under all that junk, but now look at you—you are beautiful, transformed, perfect."

4. Paul asks that their "love may abound more and more in knowledge and depth of insight" (v. 9) so that they "may be able to discern what is best," that they "may be pure and blameless until the day of Christ" (v. 10), and be "filled with the fruit of righteousness that comes through Jesus Christ," all for the "glory and praise of God" (v. 11). This fruit of righteousness imitates Christ through our dying to ourselves, becoming servants, and emptying ourselves (2:6–11). It is not from us, but from

Jesus. Thus, this righteousness is ultimately God's work and will bring glory to him. The only righteousness that counts is what God produces in our lives. With any other righteousness, the praise goes elsewhere rather than to God.

5–6. Answers will vary.

7. Before you know it, you will be at the end of your life saying, "Wow! Didn't that go fast?" Life in this world is like the morning mist that appears for a short time and then is gone. One second of the new heaven and earth will outweigh seventy years of suffering. Those who live for this world sometimes say, "Things are not so bad." God, however, says, "Oh yes, they are. Life here is difficult, painful, confusing, and miserable because of sin. But I have something far better in mind for you. What I have planned for you will overwhelm this present suffering. Of course your troubles are heavy, but I am giving you something far heavier—a weight of glory so great, it cannot be compared with your sufferings." At the end of his life D. L. Moody wrote, "Someday you will read in the papers that D. L. Moody, of east Northfield, is dead. Don't you believe a word of it! At that moment I shall be more alive than I am now, I shall have gone up higher, that is all." Knowing our ultimate end, and knowing Christ has promised to bring us there, frees us to be who God has already created us to be in Christ.

8–12. Answers will vary. Encourage your group to spend more time on this activity during the week—recording (and celebrating) what God has done, reflecting on God's goodness and presence, asking God "Where are we going next?" and submitting their lives to his direction and purpose, knowing that he will be with them even unto the end of this age (Matthew 28:20)—and into eternity.

SESSION 10: ~~DYING~~ LIVING DAILY IN JESUS

1–2. Answers will vary.

3. We don't want to die. We don't want to lose what little we have—what we call ours—even though everything we have comes from God. Even the "being given over" part *hurts*. But the fact is that we have not died with

Christ because we *think* we have, or because we *agree* that we have. We *have* died with Christ. Our old life is done. And we need to truly *realize* that and live in that new reality.

4. Dying daily is the way we experience the power of Christ's resurrection—power made perfect in weakness. We find life in dying. More than that, others find life through our dying (2 Corinthians 4:12), and this leads us to joy. Jesus endured the cross (Hebrews 12:2), for it meant life for others. Through Paul's sufferings, many were brought to life. This way of living brought joy to Paul, and he calls others to rejoice with him. Paul died daily in that he considered all things loss for the sake of knowing Christ. Paul died daily in suffering for the benefit of others.

5. Personal examples will vary. This idea of laying down your lives for Christ's sake is both foundational and eternal. It's how we first come to Jesus, and it's how Jesus continues to shape our will in union with his. Our lives move from being *of* Christ to being "*in* Christ" (Ephesians 1:3; 2:10) to where finally our life "*is* Christ" (2 Corinthians 4:10; Galatians 2:20; Philippians 1:21; 2:12–15; Colossians 3:4).

6. We are to love as Christ loved us, so that our joy may be full. We are only able to love because Jesus first loved us (1 John 4:19). We show our love by laying down our lives for others. This love is nothing less than dying. We must recognize that true love leads to dying. Love, properly understood, brings death into our lives. Death for someone is the greatest example of love.

7. Often, we are like Peter and think we can easily lay down our lives for Christ. Jesus, however, asks Peter, "Will you really lay down your life for me?" In other words, the question to Peter is, "Will you really die to your fear of other people?" The question Jesus asks of Peter he asks of us: "Will you really lay down your life?" Will we die to our love for status, for control, for food, for drink, for sex, for our own ambitions, for our career, for television, for possessions, for our own reputation and status? Will we lay down our pleasures for the sake of Christ, so that we can love? If we are not dying daily, our Christian "talk" is only a substitute for true Christian discipleship.

8. We will meet hostility with loving forgiveness. We will love our enemies and pray for our persecutors. We will love one another in the new

community. We will not retaliate for insults and threats. Judging will be replaced by compassion and honesty. Think about Jesus' compassion for the Samaritan woman, lepers, and prostitutes—people no self-respecting person would be caught dead with. Who would ever have associated with a sinful Samaritan woman (John 4)? Who would ever have reached out and touched a leper (Mark 1:41)? Who would ever have let a prostitute touch him (Luke 7:38)? Because the Pharisees and experts in the law were not willing to die to themselves, they kept themselves from being in relationship with others. Jesus' life was the exact opposite of theirs. If we die daily, as he did, we will remove the barriers that separate us from other people, especially from the despised and rejected.

9. Again, dying to self is difficult. It's *dying*, after all. But we are promised a resurrection body and life that is imperishable, powerful, spiritual, immortal. We will finally fully represent God's image.

10. To obtain life, we must die. It is in his dying that Jesus supremely glorifies God. Similarly, we primarily glorify God as we die daily. We do not glorify God through our great programs, buildings, activities, or ministries, but in dying for each other. Dying daily is not just about releasing our bad stuff, but also offering up everything "good" we have to God. Jesus, the ultimate good, offered himself up for us. Who are we to do less, and why do we think the ultimate results would not be as glorious?

Therefore, we don't stop working, but we make it about "working for the Lord" (Colossians 3:23). We're still parents and children and spouses and friends, but our priority becomes glorifying God in those relationships rather than pleasing ourselves, or even that spouse or parent or child or friend. We still use our gifts and talents, but we do so to serve God fully and not just for ego fulfillment—even, or maybe especially, in the context of "doing God's work." We still receive amazing blessings from God, but we learn to immediately place them back in God's hands, knowing that even the people and things we love most are given to us for *his* purposes, and that our joy must rest in that rather than in his gifts.

11. Answers will vary.

mission

grace through you

At Serge we believe that mission begins through the gospel of Jesus Christ bringing God's grace into the lives of believers. It also sustains us and empowers us to go into different cultures bringing the good news of forgiveness of sins and new life to those whom God is calling to himself.

As a cross-denominational, reformed, sending agency with 200 missionaries on over 25 teams in 5 continents, we are always looking for people who are ready to take the next step in sharing Christ, through:

- **Short-term Teams:** One to two-week trips oriented around serving overseas ministries while equipping the local church for mission

- **Internships:** Eight-week to nine-month opportunities to learn about missions through serving with our overseas ministry teams

- **Apprenticeships:** Intensive 12–24 month training and ministry opportunities for those discerning their call to cross-cultural ministry

- **Career:** One- to five-year appointments designed to nurture you for a lifetime of ministry

 Grace at the Fray   Visit us online at: www.whm.org/go

www.newgrowthpress.com

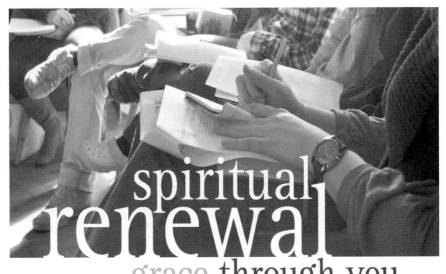

spiritual renewal
grace through you

Disciples who are motivated and empowered by grace to reach out to a broken world are handmade, not mass-produced. Serge intentionally grows disciples through curriculum, discipleship experiences, and training programs.

Curriculum for Every Stage of Growth

Serge offers grace-based, gospel-centered studies for every stage of the Christian journey. Every level of our materials focuses on essential aspects of how the Spirit transforms and motivates us through the gospel of Jesus Christ.

- 101: The Gospel-Centered Series
  (The Gospel-Centered Life, The Gospel-Centered Community)

- 201: The Gospel Transformation Series
  (Gospel Identity, Gospel Growth, Gospel Love)

- 301: The Sonship Course and Serge Individual Mentoring

Gospel Renewal for You

For over 25 years Serge has been discipling ministry leaders around the world through our Sonship course to help them experience the freedom and joy of having the gospel transform every part of their lives. A personal discipler will help you apply what you are learning to the daily struggles and situations you face, as well as, modeling what a gospel-centered faith looks and feels like.

Training to Help You Disciple Better

Serge's discipler training programs have been refined through our work with thousands of people worldwide to help you gain the biblical understanding and practical wisdom you need to disciple others so they experience substantive, lasting growth in their lives. Available for onsite training or via distance learning, our training programs are ideal for ministry leaders, small group leaders or those seeking to grow in their ability to disciple effectively.

 Grace at the Fray   Visit us online at www.whm.org/grow

www.newgrowthpress.com

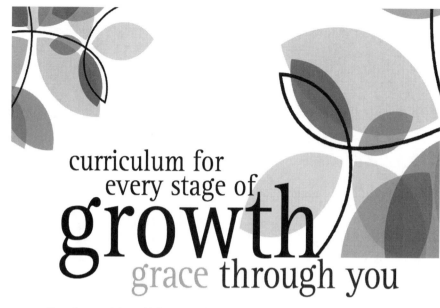

curriculum for
every stage of
growth
grace through you

Every day around the world, Serge teams help people develop and deepen the living, breathing, growing relationship with Jesus that the gospel promises. We help people connect with God in ways that are genuinely grace-motivated and that increase their desire and ability to reach out to others. No matter where you are along the way, we have a series that is right for you.

101: The *Gospel-Centered* Series

Our *Gospel-Centered* series is simple, deep, and transformative. Each *Gospel-Centered* lesson features an easy-to-read article and provides challenging discussion questions and application questions. Best of all, no outside preparation on the part of the participants is needed! They are perfect for small groups, those who are seeking to develop "gospel DNA" in their organizations and leaders, and contexts where people are still wrestling with what it means to follow Jesus.

201: The *Gospel Transformation* Series

Our *Gospel Transformation* studies take the themes introduced in our 101 level materials and expand and deepen them. Designed for those seeking to grow through directly studying Scripture and working through rich exercises and discussion questions, each *Gospel Transformation* lesson helps participants grow in the way they understand and experience God's grace. Ideal for small groups, individuals who are ready for more, and one-on-one mentoring, *Gospel Identity*, *Gospel Growth*, and *Gospel Love* provide substantive material, in easy-to-use, manageable sized studies.

The *Sonship* Course and Individual Mentoring from Serge

Developed for use with our own missionaries and used for over 25 years with thousands of Christian leaders in every corner of the world, Sonship sets the standard for whole-person, life transformation through the gospel. Designed to be used with a mentor, or in groups ready for a high investment with each other and deep transformation, each lesson focuses on the type of "inductive heart study" that brings about change from the inside out.

 Grace at the Fray   Visit us online at www.whm.org/bookstore

www.newgrowthpress.com